POLICY AND PRACTICE IN EDUCATION

EDITORS

GORDON KIRK *AND* ROBERT GLAISTER

COMMUNITY EDUCATION, LIFELONG LEARNING AND SOCIAL INCLUSION

Lyn Tett

DUNEDIN ACADEMIC PRESS

EDINBURGH

Published by
Dunedin Academic Press Ltd
Hudson House
8 Albany Street
Edinburgh EH1 3QB
Scotland

ISBN 1 903765 11 0

British Library Cataloguing in Publication Data

A catalogue record for this book is available from the British Library

Typeset by Trinity Typing, Wark on Tweed
Printed in Great Britain by Cromwell Press

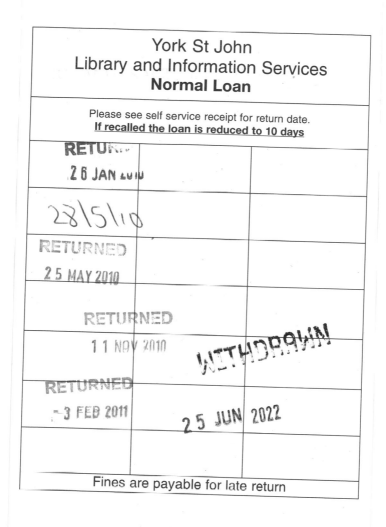

York St John
Library and Information Services
Normal Loan

Please see self service receipt for return date.
If recalled the loan is reduced to 10 days

RETURN 2 6 JAN 2010		
28\5\10		
RETURNED 2 5 MAY 2010		
RETURNED 1 1 NOV 2010	WITHDRAWN	
RETURNED -3 FEB 2011	2 5 JUN 2022	

Fines are payable for late return

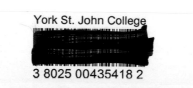

POLICY AND PRACTICE IN EDUCATION

CONTENTS

EDITORIAL INTRODUCTION

Education is now widely regarded as having a key contribution to make to national prosperity and to the well-being of the community. Arguably, of all forms of investment in the public good, it deserves the highest priority. Given the importance of education, it is natural that it should be the focus of widespread public interest and that the effectiveness and responsiveness of the educational service should be of vital concern to politicians, teachers and other professionals, parents and members of the general public. If anything, the establishment of Scotland's parliament, which has already affirmed education as a key priority, will witness an intensification of public interest in the nature and direction of educational policy and the changing practices in the schools. This series of books on *Policy and Practice in Education* seeks to support the public and professional discussion of education in Scotland.

In recent years there have been significant changes in every aspect of education in Scotland. The series seeks to counter the tendency for such changes to be under-documented and to take place without sufficient critical scrutiny. While it will focus on changes of policy and practice in Scotland, it will seek to relate developments to the wider international debate on education.

Each volume in the series will focus on a particular aspect of education, reflecting upon the past, analysing the present, and contemplating the future. The contributing authors are all well established and bring to their writing an intimate knowledge of their field, as well as the capacity to offer a readable and authoritative analysis of policies and practices.

The author of this volume, the fourth in the series, is Professor Lyn Tett, Director of Community Education at Moray House Institute of Education from 1992 to 1998, and now Head of the Department of Higher and Community Education in the Faculty of Education at The University of Edinburgh, following the merger of Moray House with the University.

Professor Gordon Kirk
Faculty of Education
The University of Edinburgh

Dr Robert T D Glaister
School of Education
The Open University

ACKNOWLEDGEMENTS

This book is dedicated to my family and particularly to my grandchildren; Dominic, Kieran, Scarlett and Lulu. Their vulnerability and wonder at the world that they have recently joined provides the inspiration for trying to make it a better place.

I would like to thank Jim Crowther and Paul Tett who read many drafts of this book and provided really useful and challenging advice and comments. I would also like to thank friends for cheerfully putting up with my absences whilst I worked on this book and colleagues and students in community education for providing inspiration not only about what community education is, but also about what it could be.

CHAPTER 1

COMMUNITY EDUCATION IN SCOTLAND

If you want flowers you must have flowers, roots and all, unless you are
satisfied with flowers made of paper and tinsel. And if you want education
you must not cut it off from the social interests in which it has its living
and perennial sources (Tawney, 1926: 22).

Introduction
In Scotland community education is currently provided both through the local
authorities and through a range of voluntary organisations and includes work with
young people, community based learning, popular adult education and community
work. Community education as now practised was not established in Scotland until
the 1970s as a result of the recommendations of the Alexander Report (SED, 1975).
Although it is one of the newest forms of educational development in Scotland, its
conceptual origins stem from two much older traditions originating in the late
eighteenth and early nineteenth centuries (see Crowther, 1999). One of these came
from the radical working class organisations that developed popular educational
activities and a curriculum that involved acting and educating against the *status
quo* in order to develop 'knowledge calculated to make you free' (Johnson, 1988).
The other tradition is derived from the philanthropic provision of adult education
and youth work for poor people in order to help alleviate their problems. These
different assumptions about the purpose, role and focus of the work derived from
these traditions are still present in community education today. The first, radical,
tradition within community education is committed to progressive social and political
change and attempts, wherever possible, to forge a direct link between education
and social action. The second, reformist, tradition leads to a community education
that has a more top-down approach that is concerned to solve the problems that
impact on the quality of life for people but is not committed to challenging dominant
ways of thinking.

Community education takes place outside of institutions and responds to the
notion of 'community'. Community is a concept that is difficult to define but it
can be broadly divided into three main areas of meaning:

- Place — this is the most common meaning and refers to people living in a
  particular geographical community such as a neighbourhood or village.
- Interest — this refers to people who share the same interest or activity such
  as community activists or environmentalists or members of the same
  religious or ethnic group

- Function — this refers to groups with the same profession, such as teachers, or the same role, such as community representatives, who acquire a common sense of identity despite not having the same physical locus.

Community education tends to mainly work with communities of place but, more broadly, sees a community as a group of people who perceive common needs and problems, have a sense of identity and a common sense of objectives. Not everyone will be fully engaged in these different types of community and its strength within any group is determined by the degree to which its members experience both a sense of solidarity and a sense of significance within it.

Education, which grows out of the experiences of ordinary people and the social interests that are generated within communities, has a different focus from mainstream education both in its curriculum and in its methods. It is about encouraging and engaging people throughout life into learning that is based on their interests. Education is developed that is enjoyable and relevant to the participating learners and is responsive to community priorities and needs identified *with* people rather than *for* them. The motivation and purpose for learning of the participants will change over time but if education is rooted in the community 'it will allow genuinely alternative and democratic agendas to emerge at the local level' (Martin, 1996:140).

The next sections will provide a short history of the development of community education in Scotland so that the assumptions behind the various policy documents and their implications for the work can be examined.

In the beginning
The Alexander Report *Adult Education: the challenge of change*, (SED, 1975) that led to the setting up of the Community Education Service in Scottish Regional and Island Authorities, was originally established to examine the role of non-vocational adult education. This was in a relatively weak position in Scotland compared to England since local authority provision had been slow to develop, perhaps because 'the long-established pattern of relatively open and democratic access to higher education diverted attention away from the development of non-vocational liberal adult education' (Martin, 1996:131). The recommendations of the Alexander Report were strongly influenced by an understanding that adult education should help to counter the disadvantage experienced by a range of groups including lone parents, unemployed people, early school leavers and minority ethnic communities. Participation in community education was expected to enable these groups and individuals to 'develop their capacities for a full and rich personal life' (SED, 1975: 26). Educational intervention should aim to minimise the impediments to participation experienced by many adults. Research commissioned by the committee found, for example, that 'those to whom education should be of most value are least involved' (SED, 1975:15).

Although adult education was relatively weak youth and community work had been significantly expanded from the later 1960s in response to the 1964 Report *Children and Young Persons in Scotland* and was a well-established part of the Scottish local authorities provision. The infrastructure of the Youth and Community Service provided a localised and responsive provision that was underpinned by a community development approach. At the time there was a widespread interest in inter-agency strategies for local service delivery. For example, the Standing Consultative Council on Youth and Community Services' report *Community of Interests* had recommended that 'within the sphere of informal further education, further development of the youth and community services [should be promoted] and... co-operation among the statutory authorities and voluntary organisations concerned [should be fostered]' (SCCYCS, 1969). These services, however, had very different ideological roots and cultural practices. Colin Kirkwood has caricatured them as:

> Adult education was organised by men in suits... who ran classes in evening institutes, usually in schools and at night.... They saw themselves as educators. The youth service was different. It was also run by male workers but they tended to be more informal, with open necked shirts. They ran youth clubs with table tennis, dancing, football and other sports (Kirkwood, 1990: 295).

However, despite their differences the Alexander Committee saw a number of pragmatic reasons why these services should be brought together. One reason was that youth and community workers were seen as being closer to the people than the traditional subject-centred and institution-based adult education service. Another was that the joining of adult education together with a numerically far stronger youth and community service, rich in buildings and staff, was expected to provide a range of contacts and understanding to which adult educators could respond. Thus the Report sought to create the conditions though which adult education could move from being the leisure pursuit of an affluent minority to becoming a more relevant and locally based enterprise that involved the mass of people who had traditionally not participated in its provision.

The key recommendation of the Report was that 'adult education should be regarded as an aspect of community education and should, with the youth and community service, be incorporated into a community education service' (SED, 1975: 35). The 'challenge of change' that it posed to this new service was to escape from the conventional syllabi of school-based evening classes that had involved less than 4% of the population, largely from its older, better educated and more affluent members. Instead the new service was to create new and relevant curricula within communities and community centres that, by their very power of appeal and relevance, would stimulate participation in education. The Report consistently argued for change and qualitative improvement and redirection rather than an expansion that was more of the same. Its focus was on involving groups that were socially, educationally and economically disadvantaged who were trapped, it was suggested, in 'a cycle of deprivation'.

The publication of the Alexander Report was timed to coincide with local government reform and the advent of the new large local authorities in Scotland. These unprecedentedly large-scale units would, it was assumed, provide an adequate resource base for the development and expansion of the new service. The Alexander recommendations reflected the approach common in state planning at that time that looked for centralisation that brought economies of scale and the advantages of strategic planning. At the same time it reflected the 'concern characteristic of the time to foster local democracy by encouraging devolution, accountability and participation at the local level' (Martin, 1996: 132). The locally based Community Education Service would, in Alexander's view, have an important part to play in nurturing a pluralist democracy by helping to manage the tension between the policies of the state and the politics of communities. These were often in conflict as the state sought to reduce public expenditure and communities sought to retain their rights. The central concern of the Report, to address issues of social and educational disadvantage, meant that the challenge for adult education was to increase its capacity to respond to the interests and needs of particular groups. These were conceived primarily in terms of those most likely to suffer the negative consequences of economic and social change and, potentially, to become more alienated and disaffected from the political process.

The outcome of the Report was the establishment, with some local variation, of an integrated Community Education Service in most of the new Scottish regional and island authorities. The work of such services was to be characterised by local community-oriented approaches with a pronounced emphasis on positive discrimination in favour of traditionally non-participant groups. Sir Kenneth Alexander, reflecting back on his committee's recommendations, confirmed that the basic intention was that adult education's use of the youth work base in communities 'should create a wider network within which more people could become aware of educational opportunities' (1993: 36). The Report conceived of adult educators and youth workers as 'committed allies' with a 'common purpose' and recommended substantial investment in new appointments, training and research in adult education. These new appointments would equalise the relationship with youth workers, who outnumbered adult educators by a ratio of seven to one (Kirkwood: 1990: 297). This requirement was never met. As a consequence, rather than identifying a 'common core of know-ledge and expertise', work was carried out in three central areas — informal educational work with young people, community based adult education and community development work. Few of the people undertaking this work had had any further professional training and so continued to work within their existing traditions. It was soon realised that if changes were to occur in practice then new forms of pre-service and in-service training had to be available.

Training for Change
The first report to address the issue of training, chaired by Lady Carnegie (SED, 1977), tried to identify the common core of knowledge and skills required by community education workers. This was a departure from the proposals made by the Alexander Report, which had argued that adult educators and youth workers had different strengths that should be built on through training. Carnegie

then diminished the strengths of the different strands of community education and emphasised instead the common core of knowledge and skills required for community education. The Report also made grand claims about community education through presenting an idealising description of what it could do.

> The significance of community education for the well being of society, for the quality of life in communities, and for the personal fulfilment of individuals is now widely recognised (SED, 1977: 7).

Such claims were clearly inflated. The service had only just started and there was no evidence of its efficacy. They were probably a way of trying to 'hype community education in order to gain extra resources in a time of economic stringency' (Kirkwood, 1990: 302). However, these grand claims meant there was the danger of a gap opening up between claim and performance so that community education might be setting itself up to fail.

The next report about training was developed by the Scottish Community Education Council and was called *Training for Change* (SCEC, 1984). In this report community education was seen as an umbrella term that had at its heart a process that involved 'purposive developmental and educational programmes and structures which afford opportunities for individual and collective growth and change throughout life' (SCEC, 1984: 3). The Report acknowledged that workers would need more in depth knowledge of particular areas of community education and one proposal was that there should be more training time spent in fieldwork practice. Generally the pattern of training proposed was to enable the community educator to fulfil a variety of roles. These included working 'as an educator, as a communicator, as a facilitator, as a manager and as a trainer of part-time and voluntary colleagues' (McConnell, 1996: 213). As well as these varied roles the Report also sketched out the range of additional responsibilities that community education had gained in the eight years since the publication of the Alexander Report. It was now covering adult basic education, vocational training, women's education, children's play, older people and community schools, as well as the original functions. *Training for Change*, in the light of all these new responsibilities, summarises community education as a 'rapidly expanding field of practice'. Surprisingly, however, the Report did not complain that few extra resources had been supplied to fulfil these increased responsibilities. It merely tried to come up with a training programme that would encompass all these areas. In order to do this the Report recommended a 'core and options model of training, in which generic training forms the core and the training in specific settings [and the broad arenas of adult education, community work and youth work] forms the options' (McConnell, 1996: 215).

Colin Kirkwood assesses the Report as reflecting the 'anxiety of the profession about the core of its identity,... and the absence of boundaries around its core business' (Kirkwood, 1990: 306). Welding together professions with very different traditions into something that has clear common objectives takes time and resources that were certainly not available to this developing service. Indeed, the Scottish Secretary of State took three years to respond to the Report and then rejected all the recommendations that would have involved providing any new resources. It is thus hardly surprising that a detailed study of practice in the Community Education Service carried out in the early 1980s by David Alexander and colleagues (Alexander et al, 1984) suggested that the development of generic approaches had negative effects on the adult education elements of the work. In their view this was mainly because the dominance of youth work traditions of non-direction and facilitative group work impeded systematic learning and cognitive development by the participants in the provision. According to Ian Martin (1996: 135) this meant that 'the educational elements of the service's work tended to be presented in covert, or at least very oblique, terms with learning seen as an incidental accretion'.

Refocusing on learning
During the 1980s the local authorities, particularly the largest such as Strathclyde, Lothian and Tayside, put more resources into community education because it was seen as taking the lead in regenerating disadvantaged communities. This led to the creation of 'a community development arm of education departments, which allowed and indeed encouraged, the identification of local need, the design of appropriate programmes and services and the engagement of local people in their delivery' (Milburn, 1999: 838). In the local authorities a consensus emerged that learning was at the heart of the community education profession, with the focus on how people could identify and challenge local issues. This process was seen as a fundamentally educational one and the gains that resulted were not only in community terms but also in personal skill and ability. Priorities switched from leisure and subject-based provision to community-based and issue-orientated provision. Community educators became more skilled at involving people in learning as well as in negotiating the content of that learning and building on what people already knew and could do. Previously unsupported groups who were hard to reach, such as young people who were contacted through street work, became included in learning opportunities. There was also a switch from more formal educational provision that took place in classes to much more informal learning that could take place through discussions and conversations with, for example, young people on street corners. The communities into which community educators intervened were usually designated as 'disadvantaged' because of their socio-economic position. However, they were conceived of as neither passive nor apathetic. Although they might be communities within which there was poverty of expectations and of income and wealth, there was certainly not a poverty of ideas, co-operative values and practical self-help.

The impact of these developments on the type of work undertaken in communities led to the establishment, in 1989, of the Scottish validation agency for the training of community educators, under the auspices of the Scottish Community Education Council. It was called the Community Education Validation and Endorsement Group (CeVe) and its remit was to develop guidelines for the validation of training courses in community education in Scotland. The group's first act was to develop another definition of community education. This was:

> Community Education is a process designed to enrich the lives of individuals and groups by engaging with people living in a geographical area, or sharing a common interest, to develop voluntarily a range of learning, action and reflection opportunities determined by their personal, social, economic and political needs (SCEC, 1990: 1).

The emphasis on process as well as outcome was because it was seen as vital that people were involved through taking action for themselves. In line with the importance given to process was a similar emphasis on the values underpinning the work of community educators. These included: the central role of education in achieving personal and community improvement and change; the importance of individual and group empowerment; the belief in a more equitable distribution of resources. This concept of community education was challenging to the profession and it led inevitably to demands for dramatic changes in the training and professional development of community educators. CeVe's guidelines for professionally qualifying training developed competencies that required community educators to:

- engage appropriately with local communities;
- develop relevant learning and educational opportunities;
- empower individuals and groups;
- organise and manage resources;
- demonstrate community education principles, purpose and values in youth work, adult education and community work settings;
- gather and use evaluative data to improve and develop programmes.

On the basis of these guidelines there was a thorough revision of the existing courses and an ordinary degree replaced the diploma as the professional qualification. This new training had to take account of a community education approach that was not solely about the delivery of a set of services. Rather, it was a mechanism whereby people were enabled to reflect on their experience and plan for further action through developing a critical awareness of the issues facing them. Professional education had to take account of the complex, unique, unstable and value-conflict-laden world of the community educator. In these situations problems have to be constructed out of uncertain and confusing situations where the key task is what Schon (1983) has called 'problem setting'. This is the dynamic process in a practice situation by which the decisions to be made, the ends to be achieved and the means of achieving these ends are determined. Where practice situations are uncertain, where ends are not always known, then the selection of the best methodology cannot be based on only one 'correct' way of doing things.

New challenges
By the mid 1990s there were over 1,500 trained and practising community educators employed by local authorities (in education departments and to a lesser extent in social work, neighbourhood, community and leisure services) and in the non-governmental voluntary sector. The professionals supported tens of thousands of part-time and voluntary staff and were involved in:

- Supporting young people and adults to return to education and training throughout life, with community-based guidance and provision, particularly for those who are disadvantaged.
- Supporting young people and adults in improving their communities, increasing self-help and voluntary community action in tackling problems
- Enhancing the ability of central and local government and other agencies to listen to the needs and concerns of local people and the consumers of services
- Assisting government and other agencies to raise awareness of issues through public education campaigns such as crime prevention, drugs awareness and environmental action
- Stimulating the effective involvement of local people in personal, social, cultural, economic and political development, helping people to participate actively in determining change.

Their task was to engage with people within geographical communities and communities of interest in order to identify needs, to motivate individuals and groups to acquire new knowledge, skills and confidence, and to promote learning that was enjoyable, relevant, accessible and empowering to the participating learners (McConnell, 1996: 3).

Less than 3% of total educational expenditure in Scottish Local Authorities went on community education at this time. The typical community educator worked within a community of several thousand people. One reason that community education attracted such a small proportion of the education budget was the lack of a legislative base. Education authorities had the power (but not the duty) to secure for their area:

> i) Voluntary part-time and full-time courses of instruction for persons over school age; ii) the provision of adequate facilities for social, cultural and recreative activities and physical education and training, either as voluntary organised activities designed to promote the educational development of persons taking part therein or as part of a course of instruction' (Further and Higher Education (Scotland) Act, 1992).

This weakness in the legislative position meant that when local government was reorganised in 1995 into small unitary authorities the provision of community education across Scotland was reduced. Some of the new authorities were wealthy but many were poorer. Few could afford the sophisticated central services of the now defunct regions. Many local authorities were forced to cut staff, close community buildings, reduce programmes and even shut down altogether some aspects of their provision such as community-based adult education. In a number of authorities the community education service and other council services were amalgamated to form new departments such as Community and Leisure Services, Neighbourhood Services, Community Services or Community Economic and Development Services. These amalgamations resulted in new department heads with different outlooks. Some did not see the work of community educators as inherently educational even though it might be life enhancing to communities (see Milburn, 1999: 844).

The impact of the reorganisation of local government on the Community Education Service generated concern both within the Scottish local authorities and the Scottish Office because they recognised that the provision of community education opportunities had declined in some areas by nearly fifty per cent. It appeared that there was a direct correlation between this reduction in staffing and the reduction in the most socially excluded groups participating in community education provision. For example, adult basic education participants declined by forty per cent between 1992 and 1996/7. It was suggested that 'the service had been influenced by providing for those who, in part, could pay; a market rather than a needs-led response' (COSLA, 1998: 7). This realisation led, in the summer of 1997, to the establishing of a task group by the Convention of Scottish Local Authorities (COSLA). The remit of the group was to 'provide guidelines for councils on strategies for delivering community education which address the statutory base of community education, current circumstances and future trends' (COSLA, 1998:3).

The Report called for community educators to adopt a more issues-focused and developmental role that was essentially about enhancing the confidence and capacity of individuals, community groups and other professional colleagues both within and outwith the local authority sector. The emphasis was to be on 'people-centred development' (COSLA, 1998: 11) that was to involve those that were most disadvantaged. The report made a number of recommendations, including a strengthened statutory duty to provide community education and for the revision of funding arrangements, but neither of these was implemented. The track record of government in failing to take on board anything that increased costs thus continued unbroken.

Another working group on the future of community education was set up in 1997 by the Scottish Office chaired by HM Senior Chief Inspector of Schools Douglas Osler. Its remit was 'to consider a national strategy for community based adult education, youth work and educational support for community development in the light of Government priorities in relation to social exclusion and lifelong learning' (Scottish Office, 1998a: 5). The two working groups collaborated and came to rather similar conclusions about community education as having a remit to 'support people to improve their personal, community, social and economic well being through creating learning opportunities within and for communities' (Scottish Office, 1998a: 13). The vision for Scotland developed by Osler was that it was a 'democratic and socially just society. Such a society should enable all of its citizens, in particular those who are socially excluded, to develop their potential to the full and to have the capacity, individually and collectively, to meet the challenge of change' (ibid. 14).

When she launched the Osler Report (in November 1998) Helen Liddell, Minister of State at the Scottish Office, said

> Community Education is about enhancing the quality of life of the individual and community as a whole. All ages and all social groups in communities across Scotland will benefit from the Government's approach

that is to move community education from the status of 'orphan' to mainstream provision. Education is this Government's number one priority and community education is at the very heart of this. It includes learning at all levels from the very basic life skills to learning for further and higher education. But it also includes learning for enjoyment and building better citizens and communities (Scottish Office, 1998b: 1–2).

The main recommendations of the Report were that:

• Community learning plans that would incorporate the contributions of voluntary and statutory providers should be produced that would include clear targets and monitoring procedures and be built from the bottom-up;
• Community education was to be accorded high priority in delivering the Government's policies on social inclusion, lifelong learning and active citizenship;
• Training for community education should be reviewed so that it contained a strong commitment to inter-disciplinary work;
• A new Scottish Office circular should be published that would firmly promote community education as an approach to education rather than a sector of it (Scottish Office, 1998a: 17).

This final recommendation was quickly followed, in April 1999, by a Circular to all the Scottish Local Authorities (SOEID, 1999). It argued that there was a need for a wide range of services to be provided that would involve community members in order to enable them to respond to the challenges facing Scotland. The Circular suggested that people should be equipped to play an active role in civic life and voluntary organisations but, if they were to do so, their needs for learning had to be clearly identified. It required local authorities and the various agencies working in communities to clarify both the contributions they could make and the learning needs which might arise as a result of various requirements for local consultation. Community Education was seen as central to meeting these learning needs.

The Circular (SOEID, 1999: 4.4) argued that the following tasks should be at the heart of community learning:

• development of core skills, including adult literacy, numeracy, use of information and communication technologies (ICT), problem-solving and working together;
• Engagement with young people to help them experience positive development — whether they are of school age or beyond. This was seen to apply particularly to those at transition stages who were, or who were at risk of, becoming alienated from society, those whose educational experience had left them dissatisfied or those whose lifestyle made them vulnerable;
• Educational support to individuals, families, people with disabilities, interest groups and communities that were endeavouring to improve the quality of their lives;

- Promotion of lifelong learning and healthier, more positive, lifestyles within the context of community and voluntary activities.

Circular 4/99 required Local Authorities to produce community learning plans that were to include both an assessment of the range of professional expertise available and procedures to ensure that staff from different service areas worked together in communities to address the learning needs associated with social inclusion, lifelong learning and citizenship. The Circular argued that community education must develop as a discipline if the skills of workers in community-based activity and their particular expertise, 'for example in work with alienated young people or in meeting the core skill requirements of adults' (*ibid.*: 5.23), were to improve.

Problems and possibilities
It should be clear from this short history of community education in Scotland that running through these policies has been a continuing debate about the role, purpose, focus and methodology of the work. There are many different approaches to community education and these have been broadly characterised as 'universal', 'reformist' and 'radical' (Martin, 1987). Each has a different implicit model of society and community and therefore different premises and strategies underpinning practice. Under the *universal* model it is assumed that there are shared values and a working consensus with a basic harmony of interests and so the community educator's role is to make universal non-selective provision for all ages and groups. Under the *reformist* model it is assumed that there is a plurality of interests with inter-group competition for resources and so selective intervention is made by the community educator to assist disadvantaged people and socially excluded areas. Under the *radical* model it is assumed that interests are in conflict because existing structures create inequality and powerlessness. In this model the community educator's intervention is based on 'developing with local people political education and social action focused on concrete issues and concerns in the community' (Martin, 1987: 25).

Underpinning all three models is an interest in education's role in improving social conditions, although the type of provision and the focus for intervention will vary depending on the particular ideology of practice. As can be seen from the various policy documents explored in this chapter, much of the focus of community education has been within the reformist tradition, with the role of combating 'disadvantage' to the fore. There is also a strong, but numerically rather small, movement amongst practitioners who operate under the radical model. From this perspective the community educator is an agent of social change, who does not separate the process of learning from the intentions of teaching. This tradition has always stood for purposeful educational intervention in the interests of social and political change: change towards more justice, equality and democracy.

From Carnegie (1977) through to Circular 4/99 (1999), community education has been expected to achieve major change in areas that have been defined as problems by the state. Generally it has been expected that these changes will be achieved without an increase in resources but through a refocused targeting. The problems identified generally relate to ideas of threat to the stability of the state or the well being of its 'good' citizens for example from threatening youth or from a disaffected 'underclass'. Because policy for community educators is generated from above in order to solve current problems rather than from below in response to needs, workers often face dilemmas about the focus of their practice. They have to strike a balance between the demands of policy and the interests of communities in ways that are not easily resolvable. This often leads to a focus solely on local issues at the expense of a broader analysis of their underlying causes. In addition there is an assumption that the people within a community are all the same rather than riven with conflict and inequalities, and thus that there is always a single set of solutions to their problems. Where this is coupled with a focus on 'disadvantage' and 'exclusion' education is seen as a vehicle for rebinding individuals back into society. From this perspective community education's task is to improve skills and help people to become more employable. Indeed it was only when it became clear that the most disadvantaged groups were no longer being involved in community education that the Scottish Office decided to remind local authorities through Circular 4/99 about their responsibilities for community education.

Another problem for community education has been a lack of a clear boundary around the discipline that would define the limits of the work it is expected to undertake. This has led to the making of both unrealistic claims as to what it can achieve on the part of its advocates and unrealistic expectations on the part of its funders. One reason for this is that, unlike school or university education, there is no middle class lobby demanding that community education services are properly funded and developed. Nor is there a statutory legislative base that ensures at least a minimum ratio of professionals to populations. Indeed given the values that some community educators espouse, of being on the side of people who are socially excluded, they may find themselves in the position of opposing their own funders, for example, by helping people to take action about the poor quality of their environment rather than just 'coping' with it. In addition, a focus on the least advantaged groups of the population coupled with a desire to make sure that the participants, rather than the professionals, get the credit for positive changes has resulted in community educators keeping a low profile about the profession's achievements.

Because community education takes place mainly in informal contexts outside of institutions and is therefore concerned primarily with local issues it is more difficult to pin down and define. It lacks a grand narrative that encompasses all its work because it depends on the local context in which it is taking place. This 'localness' also makes it difficult to measure its long-term impact on people's lives. This means that workers are faced with the choice of using the easy, if not unproblematic, head count of participants or trying to assess the more difficult longer-term changes. Community education then tries to justify itself in terms of numbers participating which are not central to its purpose of trying to engage the most hard-to-reach groups on terms that make sense to them. Part of this problem lies in questions about the curriculum, where it comes from, who it serves and what it implies for the community educator's role. Building a curriculum with learners is more time consuming and risky than providing a menu of choices from which participants take their pick. However, typical performance measures mean that a pre-set curriculum is easier to justify and implement. This focus on measurable achievement also leads to a tendency to go for quick-fix solutions that might alleviate the problem in the short-term but do not deal with the underlying causes. Responding to communities, however, requires the recognition that the identification of issues involves a long-term process of dialogue and negotiation between educators and prospective learners. 'As such it provides a clear rationale for reaching out to communities beyond educational institutions and for moving beyond conventional constructions of knowledge' (Johnston, 2000: 15).

Conclusion
This chapter has provided a short history of community education in Scotland and shown how its roots come from much older traditions. Recently, the Government has identified the key role for community education as addressing the learning needs of disadvantaged individuals and communities. However, it has been argued that there are ambiguities at the heart of governmental policies that have led to political and ethical choices for workers. Whilst it has been suggested that education that is rooted in the interests and experience of ordinary people can contribute to a more inclusive and democratic society it has also been shown how difficult this task is, especially when educators must react to policy generated 'from above'. Community educators have the potential to respond in a variety of ways to policies and it is important that they are clear about their purpose in intervening in communities. Community education's distinctive epistemology and methodology, that uses the lived experience of people in communities to build the learning curriculum, may simply reinforce the *status quo* if workers are not self-critical about the implementation of their practice.

Because of the importance of engaging critically with the current policy context the next chapter will explore the important policy area of lifelong learning. The focus will be on how this has been conceptualised and what the implications are for community education. Whilst the underlying values and policy reference points of lifelong learning are different from those of community education, there is sufficient common ground with its aims, starting points and methods for a useful interchange to be developed (see Johnston, 2000).

CHAPTER 2

LIFELONG LEARNING, THE LEARNING SOCIETY POLICIES AND COMMUNITY EDUCATION

> A new process of social stratification is now setting apart the segment of the highly skilled workforce who find well-paid, stable and guaranteed employment (the new nobility of excellent ability, education and competence) from all the remainder, mostly individuals with no or only limited skills, who at best might have the chance of getting a precarious, poorly paid and socially stigmatised job (Petronella, 1997: 24).

Introduction
This Scottish Parliament has placed education at the heart of its policies and identified community education as having a key role in addressing the learning needs of individuals and communities. In particular the policies that had been developed to promote lifelong learning, social inclusion and active citizenship were to be implemented by community educators, working in partnership with a range of other public, private and voluntary organisations. This chapter traces the rise of lifelong learning up the policy agenda, identify the underlying assumptions that are made and the implications of these for community educators. The importance of this task is illustrated by the above quotation because it demonstrates the dilemma posed by trying to address learning needs through creating a learning society. Whilst a commitment to the development of lifelong learning brings many opportunities for growth, development and fulfilment, without careful policy intervention, it can also serve to reinforce inequalities.

In the past there was a clear distinction made between schooling that was a preparation for adult life and post-school education that was 'either to provide compensation for inadequate or incomplete schooling or with learning that is somehow distinctive of adulthood' (Field and Leicester, 2000: xvi). 'Lifelong Learning', however, cuts across this school and post-school distinction to suggest a learning process that spans the whole of one's life. The term is also used widely to blur the boundaries between learning for work (vocational), learning for citizenship (political), learning for personal development (liberal) and learning that encourages participation in education by previously excluded groups (social). Such blurring, however, can mean that rather than all these aspects having equal importance the vocational takes precedence and the other aspects become less important. How lifelong learning and the learning society are conceptualised, then, has major implications for policy.

Lifelong Learning and conceptualisations of the learning society

The individual's capacity for learning across the life-span means that people can learn in many different ways and contexts. If the society in which they live regards learning as a normal activity for people of all ages then everyone, rather than a limited group, is likely to be effectively engaged in some form of learning of their choice. Currently, however, participation in post school education and training in the UK is a highly classed activity with those from social classes IV and V unlikely to continue their education and those from social classes I and II over-represented, particularly in Higher Education (see Tuckett and Sargant, 1999). Since those who leave school with few or no qualifications are unlikely to engage in learning later it appears that if you do not succeed in the first place then you will not succeed later either. Participation is also highly gendered where 'men... receive a greater share of substantial employer-funded education and training for adults' (Sargant et al 1997: 21). On the other hand, women out-number men by 2.5 to 1 in community based adult education classes (Sargant et al op cit) especially in Scotland, where a range of community-based adult learning initiatives succeed in engaging with women, often offering a first step back into education (see SCEC, 1995).

There are many ways in which a learning society and notions of lifelong learning could be conceptualised. For example, Robert Owen, in the nineteenth century, suggested that 'any general character, from the worst to best, from the most ignorant to the most enlightened, may be given to any community by application of [good education]' (Silver, 1965: 61). Owen regarded learning as a fundamental right of all citizens, whatever their age, and saw it as a key way of developing a more equitable society. Today the idea of a learning society has three models about what its key purpose should be: learning for work, learning for citizenship and learning for democracy (Ranson, 1998).

The world of work is being transformed by structural changes including the use of new information technologies, re-location of labour-intensive industries to low-wage economies, the shift from manufacturing to services, the intensification of international competition and the growth of part-time, intermittent employment. A view of the learning society that prioritises learning for work sees its main task as enabling employees to become more adaptable to a greater variety of occupational tasks. As the Confederation of British Industry suggested 'only by learning throughout life can individuals maintain their employability and organisations their competitive advantage' (CBI, 1991:2).

The 'learning for citizenship' approach broadens the narrow conception of the learning society which concentrates only on skills for work. A much more enriched conception of work and wealth creation is argued for, which includes the quality of people's social, cultural and political life as well as the development of their vocational skills. Moreover, 'rethinking the nature of work cannot be separated from the social and cultural relations (between the sexes, races and generations) which define who works and thus the social conditions of economic growth' (Ranson, 1998: 27).

The 'learning for democracy' approach starts from a concern to make sense of the economic, social and political transformations that have occurred and to create a learning society that would be at the centre of change. Such change requires a renewed commitment to learning that leads to a revitalised sense of democratic and social purpose. From this perspective a learning society would have at its heart the qualities of:

> Being open to new ideas, listening as well as expressing perspectives, reflecting on and inquiring into solutions to new dilemmas, co-operating in the practice of change and critically reviewing it (Ranson, 1998: 28).

These differing perspectives have major implications for the work of community educators. Community education can offer an integrated structure for the promotion of lifelong learning that takes positive action to enable excluded people and communities to participate in education and training. However, the opportunities that there are for community educators to promote a learning society that is for everyone, and does not waste the creativity and knowledge of many of its citizens, are constrained by the way in which the learning society is conceptualised. The next part of this chapter examines some of the European, UK and Scottish policies on lifelong learning in order to identify ways in which they might be exploited that would promote a more inclusive society.

Lifelong learning policies
Policies about lifelong learning were first developed in Europe and the UK in the early 1990s. Although there had been a number of policy documents produced by UNESCO and the OECD in the 1970s the idea of lifelong learning only entered the mainstream political vocabulary when it was adopted by the European Union (EU) as a key priority. Since the Treaty of Rome the EU had some legal competence in vocational training, but, following the Maastricht Treaty (1992), it also acquired legal competence in the education policies of the member states. This meant it was able to pursue two of its prime objectives of achieving economic and social cohesion and shifting attitudes to both education and training through a focus on lifelong learning (see Field, 2000). These policies became fully operationalised in 1996 when this was declared as the 'European Year of Lifelong Learning', and have been taken up and developed by UK and Scottish governments since.

Policies, as Ball (1990:22) has argued, are 'statements about practice — the ways things could or should be — which are derived from statements about the world'. What is seen as legitimate in terms of policy and practice privileges certain visions and interests which embody claims to speak with authority in ways that shut out alternatives. A particular conception of what the problem is, and consequently how it is to be solved, becomes dominant and that makes it difficult to see that there are alternatives. So if the problem facing governments is conceptualised as being about employment and training then solutions that prioritise the development of vocational skills follow. If governments see their main task as responding to an economic and employment climate where mobility and short term contracts have become the norm, with the concomitant need to constantly update knowledge and skills, then they will prioritise learning for work. This leads to a debate that emphasises the economic importance of knowledge and suggests that the 'information and knowledge based revolution of the twenty-first century [will be based] on investment in the intellect and creativity of people' (DfEE, 1998: 9).

However, although the conception of lifelong learning and the learning society as evidenced through these policies may be limited to learning for work, the potential exists for those community educators who are committed to a social justice agenda to interpret the policies more radically. One particular issue has been the prevailing orthodoxy that privileges the view that education must be modernised and become more response to the needs of employers. From this perspective education becomes the mere instrument of the economy. As the Prime Minister put it 'Education is the best economic policy we have' (Blair, 1998: 9). Such a view of society denigrates the values of caring and mutual support and values the economic over the social. It also excludes those people who are not part of the 'normal' labour market such as retired people or those who are caring for young children or those with disabilities that prevent them from working.

It is now appropriate to examine some of the key EU, UK and Scottish policy documents on lifelong learning in order to explore how the policy debate has been constrained through the imposition of particular political discourses.

A European Union Perspective
At EU level the term 'Lifelong Learning' first came into common parlance in the 1994 White Paper *'Growth, Competitiveness, Employment: the Challenges and Ways Forward into the 21st Century'* (CEC: 1994). As the title suggests, the paper was primarily concerned with laying out a formula for economic success within the Union. However, within the introduction, the Paper recognises 'lifelong education and training' as key to job retention and economic prosperity. It goes on to say:

> Our countries' education and training systems are faced with major difficulties... [that] are rooted in social ills [such as] the breakdown of the family and the demotivation bred by unemployment. Preparation for life in tomorrow's world cannot be satisfied by once-and-for-all acquisition of knowledge and know how... All measures must therefore necessarily be based on the concept of developing, generalising and systematising lifelong learning and continuous training (CEC 1994: 16, 146).

These paragraphs enshrine many of the key concepts underpinning the European paradigm of lifelong learning. The diagnosis of the problem facing the European Union was that it faced the threats and opportunities of globalisation, information technology and the application of science but these could be best dealt with by pooling some of their sovereignty and resources in education and training (see Field, 2000). In order to achieve this member states were asked to develop policies that met the education and training needs created by long-term unemployment. The paper suggested that this would be most effectively achieved if the delivery mechanisms used were increasingly flexible and if the management of education systems were increasingly decentralised. This view emphasises the value of competitiveness between education and training institutions where decentralised institutions compete with each other to provide the best services. It also values the ability of the intending participant to chose from amongst a range of providers and from different kinds of provision such as open learning, e-learning as well as face-to-face education. With such a strong focus on the providers of learning little attention is given to learners and the circumstances that effect their learning. This means that the willingness and ability to participate in continuing education and training is treated unproblematically and it is assumed that, if the supply is there, then demand will follow.

In terms of society and its social cohesion the paper provides an unreflective and somewhat pathological view of 'the family' that has apparently 'broken down'. The consequences of this breakdown are not carefully explored but there is a strong implication that the range of social ills such as delinquency, vandalism, child abuse, that beset society can be alleviated by reforming the family rather than other aspects of society. In this analysis there is an implicit separation of the problems presented by individuals from the social and political order that created the problems and a blaming of women for not prioritising their families' needs. In many ways this approach mirrors that popularised by Etzioni (1993: 61) whose argument is that the decline of the two-parent family lies at the heart of the problems of western society because both parents are necessary to provide mutually supportive educational involvement if children are to learn effectively.

The stated aim of a second White Paper, *'Teaching and Learning towards the Learning Society'* (CEC, 1995) was to address what were perceived as 'factors of upheaval' affecting member states. These were identified as the impact of the information society, the impact of internationalisation as it affects job creation, and the impact of the scientific and technical worlds. These were similar to those identified in 1994 but this paper also prioritised education and training concerned with citizenship, personal fulfilment and the tackling of exclusion. This was an important development but the analysis of social exclusion was of a process that happened once and for all. Social exclusion was not seen as a cumulative process that could be compounded by the new emphasis that was placed on having knowledge when those who are deemed unskilled are further marginalised. Just as income inequality polarises the poor from the rich, so the generalisation of lifelong learning could increase the isolation of non-participants from the world of the 'knowledge rich'.

A third White Paper, *'Learning for Active Citizenship'* was published in 1998. It suggested:

> In a high-technology knowledge society... learners must become proactive and more autonomous, prepared to renew their knowledge continuously

and to respond constructively to changing constellations of problems and contexts (CEC, 1998: 9).

Here the emphasis was on the learner becoming pro-active and acquiring the skills and habits of self-regulation and self-monitoring. The learners were seen as individuals, separated from society as a whole, so if they failed to participate in the new learning opportunities they could be blamed for not making the most of the chances they were given. These assumptions become mechanisms for legitimating inequalities — inequalities that 'may themselves be arising partly from the general acceptance of the idea and practice of lifelong learning' (Field, 2000:104).

In October 2000 the Commission issued a working paper '*Memorandum of Lifelong Learning*' (CEC, 2000). In it they stated that there were 'two equally important aims for lifelong learning: promoting active citizenship and promoting employability'. They continued by arguing that 'both employability and active citizenship are dependent on having adequate and up-to-date knowledge and skills to take part in and make a contribution to economic and social life' (ibid.: 5). Although this paper widened learning by including social life there was an absence of other purposes such as personal or community development. There was also no acknowledgement that 'adults bring something that derives both from their experience of adult life and from their status as citizens to the educational process. Adult education constructs knowledge and does not merely pass it on' (Jackson (1995: 187). Learners were constructed as empty vessels to be filled with knowledge and skills by others that were also able to pre define their needs, with the individual having little input to this process.

UK and Scottish Government Perspectives
In December 1995 a consultative document on Lifetime Learning was introduced for the first time in the UK. While issues of lifelong learning had been raised in other government policies, this was the first coherent view of government's vision of lifelong learning. The primary concern was with economic competitiveness and human resource development. However, like its European counterpart, it also recognised the importance of learning in other spheres:

> The presentation and acquisition of knowledge and the ability of individuals to fulfil their personal capacity are vital signs of a free and civilised society (DfEE 1995: 4).

Despite this wider vision learning was seen as responding to market forces. An example of this was the major roles and responsibilities ascribed to individuals and the minor role ascribed to government:

- First, the learning market should be driven by customers and their choices, not by providers or other organisations;
- Second, demand for learning should be well informed and the result of considered plans;

- Third, the government should intervene only where it can effectively lower the barriers that prevent the learning market working properly or accelerate the introduction of good practice; it should not seek to distort decisions on learning.
- Public expenditure needs to be justified in terms of wider economic and social returns (DfEE. 1995: 40).

The consultative document embodied an assumption that it was the responsibility of the individual to engage with the learning society and the underpinning ideas were about pragmatic expediency and market principles rather than any wider egalitarian understanding. This was made even clearer by a Scottish Office document issued in 1997 that stated, 'Scotland's future competitiveness demands a more highly skilled and adaptable work force. To achieve this we must convince individuals of the relevance of continuing learning' (SOEID, 1997: 5).

In February 1998 the New Labour Administration issued a Green Paper 'The Learning Age'. It again reiterated the need 'for a well-educated, well-equipped and adaptable labour force' (DfEE, 1998: 3) but added '[learning] helps make ours a civilised society, develops the spiritual side of our lives and promotes active citizenship. It strengthens the family, the neighbourhood and consequently the nation' (ibid.). Throughout the paper there was an emphasis on partnership, with the government's role 'to help create a framework of opportunities for people to learn' [by] sharing responsibility with employers, employees and the community' (p6). This was followed by 'Opportunity Scotland' (Scottish Executive, 1998a) which paralleled the concerns of the DfEE paper. In both these documents, whilst there was a clear shift from the earlier emphasis on the primacy of the market, the obstacles posed by class, poverty, employment status and gender were not explored.

When there was a concern about those who were excluded, rather than appealing to social solidarity, there was an emphasis on the threat to the established certainties. Thus the UK government's National Advisory Council on Education and Training Targets warned in 1998 that:

> Social exclusion is expensive, not merely because of the burden that it imposes on the social security system, but also because of the indirect costs that arise from, for example, juvenile delinquency and the greater levels of ill-health that poorer members of society suffer (NACETT, 1998: 13).

These sentiments were paralleled in the Scottish Consultation Paper '*Skills for Scotland: a Skills Strategy for a Competitive Scotland*' (Scottish Executive, 1999). Yet Scottish policy already included a much broader understanding of the importance of inclusion because of its commitment to social justice, as can be seen from the following.

> Those of us who benefit from the opportunities of life in modern Scotland have a duty to seek to extend similar opportunities to those who do not. Social exclusion is unacceptable in human terms; it is also wasteful, costly and carries risks in the long term for our social cohesion and well being.

This Government is determined to take action to tackle exclusion, and to develop policies which will promote a more inclusive, cohesive and ultimately sustainable society (Scottish Executive, 1998b: 1).

However, in both countries the perceived associations between exclusion and anti-social behaviour made it easy to justify the compulsory requirement to participate in vocational training under the 'New Deal' regulations. Adults who were seen as being 'at risk' required experts to help them deal with their problems 'appropriately' (Scottish Executive, 2000a). Moreover, as John Field points out, (2000: 111) 'the fact that individuals are treated as though they can acquire and understand the implications of new information about their well being becomes in turn a *justification* for reducing public services'.

If the assumptions contained in these policies are to be challenged then it is important to identify a framework for critically analysing their contradictions so that opportunities for more radical action can be identified. Policies about lifelong learning draw on a number of inter-related fallacies that cumulatively give the impression of a commitment to lifelong learning only in relation to its economic value. However, if these fallacies are separated out and examined it becomes easier to see how they might be challenged by those who are committed to a more radical view. In order to do this the next section explores each in turn.

Fallacy: Education and training are commodities in the market

The policies outlined above place education and training within the market place and regard it as a commodity that can be bought and sold like any other good. From this perspective failures in education are assumed to be because the 'producers' of education and training have taken over and pursue their own purposes at the expense of the needs of the 'consumers' of the service. Marketisation and the commodification of public services are thus portrayed as mechanisms that, through the promotion of competition, lead to greater efficiency and increased consumer control. The overt claim is that such policies will bring about an improvement in the quality of educational provision by creating a system in which high quality provision is financially rewarded. However, the covert aim is to undermine the power of those professionals who appear to stand in the way of competition.

There is little empirical evidence, however, to suggest that removal of the power of professionals and the placing of education and training within a market context does improve efficiency or user control. For example, the incorporation of Further Education Colleges, which increased competition and discouraged partnership, led to fewer opportunities for socio-economically excluded individuals and communities rather than more (see Tett and Ducklin, 1995). This research showed that colleges became less responsive to the education and training opportunities that were asked for by marginalised communities because these opportunities were expensive to provide. Instead, colleges were more likely to present a menu of existing courses from which learners were expected to pick. Rather than empowering consumers a market driven system perpetuates inequalities because, as Stewart Ranson suggests:

The market elides, but reproduces, the inequalities that consumers bring to the market place. Under the guise of neutrality, the institution of the market actively confirms and reinforces the pre-existing social class order of wealth and privilege (Ranson, 1994: 95–96).

In a class-divided society this process of 'marketisation' means that 'cultures which give primacy to the values of community and locality' lose out in the 'scramble for educational opportunity based on individual opportunity and choice' (Bowe et al, 1993: 14). This is because they do not have the financial and cultural capital to be 'active and strategic' choosers. For those marginalised by poverty or geography, their choice will be limited by the lack of accessible provision; for those marginalised by cultural difference, excluded from current systems, it will be their lack of knowledge and understanding of the system itself that disadvantages them. There seems little likelihood that the market will do anything to improve people's dispositional barriers to learning. As Keith Jackson (1995: 191) points out, 'education is a form of human exchange, which, if it is to be effective, re-quires participants to be creative partners'.

Similarly, this argument suggests that within the market context, education and training are activities which will enhance the individual's ability to engage only in economic life and through this contribute to 'national culture and quality of life' (DfEE. 1995: 3). Once the citizen is constructed primarily as a consumer a very particular and limiting notion of lifelong learning follows. Moreover, there is an emphasis on the individual that appears to militate against a desire to work with and for others. At the centre of the marketisation model is the idea of self-interested individuals as people with rights to control both their own selves and their own property free from coercion and restraint. This characterisation of human beings as by nature possessively self-interested is encouraged by the market approach. An intrinsically selfish motivation and competition are assumed because people are not seen as contributors to the democratic society which includes freedom to constrain individual action for the greater good of the whole community.

Fallacy: Economic success equals eradication of deprivation and exclusion
Within the policies outlined above inadequate skill levels within the unemployed population were seen as the causes of poverty and learning was identified as the way out of this trap. Knowledge, skills and learning were regarded as the fundamental underpinnings of life in the modern world and for an active life in communities. It follows that education and training must be modernised and become more responsive to the needs of employers since otherwise they will not meet the needs of the economy which will have benefits for all. However, the link between education and training and economic development is complex and there is little evidence that participating in learning will necessarily lead to greater prosperity for all. For example, Levin and Kelley (1997: 241), in their review of research in the USA, found that 'test scores have never shown a strong connection with either earnings or productivity'. Rather, they found that if education was to be effective for economic development it was crucially

dependent on complementary inputs from business and government. These inputs included new investment, new methods of production and of organising work, new technologies, industrial relations based on trust, sufficient customers able to buy high quality services and new managerial approaches.

These arguments that equate participation in learning with economic success also ignore the sharpening polarisation in income and wealth that can lead to a fundamental split in societies. Indeed, as the Select Committee on Education and Employment (1999) pointed out, 'a side effect of the substantial improvement in overall participation [in education] during the last two decades has been to widen the gap between the educational haves and the have-nots'. Whilst paid work is seen as the best way of averting poverty and social exclusion at the same time, if people are to be treated in relation to their potential contribution to the market economy, then a value is attached to each individual according to that contribution. 'So people with learning difficulties may come to be seen as a poor investment, more expensive to train, less flexible and less employable' (Coffield, 1999: 485). In these ways social exclusion, defined by the CEC (1993) as: 'the multiple and changing factors resulting in people being excluded from the normal exchanges, practices and rights of modern society' is intensified rather than reduced.

A final issue relating to the notion of economic success is the impact of globalisation which is generally presented as a twin process of cross-border corporate expansion and intensifying global competition, in which the world's training and manufacturing activities are woven increasingly closer together (Ritzer, 2000). One impact of this has been to see the nation-state as having diminishing powers and so there is little opportunity to intervene except through promoting education and training as a source of sustainable competition. As Frank Coffield (1999: 480) argues, this leads to the assumption that the 'new economic forces unleashed by globalisation and technology are as uncontrollable as natural disasters and so governments have no choice but to introduce policies to 'upskill' their workforce'. Such a view forgets that skills are not neutral but are socially constructed by, for example, trade unions negotiating higher pay for those jobs that are held predominantly by male members or employers offering good quality education and training only to their permanent, highly paid employees.

Fallacy: Failure is the fault of the individual
This fallacy is intimately related to the preceding two. Given that the market is perceived as fair and equal, then failure to succeed in a market structure cannot be the fault of the system, but rather is rooted in the failings of the individual to engage appropriately. Within the policy frameworks offered for lifelong learning issues such as non-participation, educational under-achievement, lack of knowledge of the range of education and training opportunities, are not perceived as structural failures but rather issues of individual attitude or ability. However, as Veronica McGivney (1990: 20) has pointed out, many adults do not participate, not because of low motivation but because of powerful constraints

that arise from cultural and social class divisions. School creates (or reinforces) sharp divisions in society, by conditioning children to accept different expectations and status patterns according to their academic 'success' or 'failure'. Through the use of imposed standards and selection, the education system traditionally rejects large numbers of the population, many of whom subsequently consider themselves as educational failures. It is hardly surprising that people do not want to engage in a process that is portrayed as 'learn or else' rather than a contribution to human flourishing.

In many ways lifelong learning is regarded as a 'moral obligation and social constraint' (Coffield, 1999: 488) by the state and employers and legitimates the shifting of the burden of responsibility for education, training and employment on to the individual. In so doing it 'implicitly denies any notion of objective structural problems such as lack of jobs, and the increasing proportion of poorly paid, untrained, routine and insecure jobs' (Darmon et al, 1999: 33). At the same time the term 'employability' also hides the tensions between training workers to meet the short-term needs of employers and the preparation for frequent changes of job for which high level general education may be more useful.

If, therefore, it is the structure of society that creates inequalities, and education and training are part of that structure, then why should individuals participate in a system in which they know they start at a disadvantage? It is insufficient simply to recognise inequality and strive for greater inclusion; rather we need to look beyond that to the causes of that inequality. Moreover, if we regard education as being about responding to individual need then no attention is paid to the ways in which these 'needs' are politically constructed and understood (see Tett, 1993). By individualising the characteristics, such as a lack of basic skills, that justify employers and others treating people differently, the trend towards lifelong learning also helps fragment the excluded and encourages a search for individual solutions. This pattern then gets reproduced through other areas of public life, such as when the welfare state switches its focus from passive support to actively inserting people back into society, the most significant strategy being through training (see Field, 2000: 111). Individuals are then assumed to be able to acquire the skills and knowledge required for them to take active responsibility for their own well-being.

The fallacy that individual failings lie at the heart of either educational failure or economic success creates a convenient scapegoat for structural inequality justified through the workings of the market. This means that the 'learning society' becomes one more way of reproducing and legitimating existing inequalities. However, as Carnoy and Levin (1985: 4) have argued, 'the relationship between education and work is dialectical — composed of a perpetual tension between two dynamics, the imperatives of capital and those of democracy in all its forms'. For far too long the economic imperative has dominated the democratic imperative and so a long struggle lies ahead for those who wish to redress the imbalance.

Fallacy: Education is neutral and ungendered

Participation in education could currently be described as a pyramid with women now predominating in continuing education and further education that are the least well-resourced sectors. As Maggie Woodrow (1996:36) points out in relation to higher education:

> In all European countries, a gender breakdown of the university system [has] at the base undergraduate level [women holding] the balance; at postgraduate level it is against them; at senior lecturer and management level they are seriously under-represented. In the education systems as a whole women are most heavily represented on the staff of primary schools and most under-represented in universities — this sector of course carrying the greatest status, remuneration and influence.

One effect of the gender imbalance amongst decision-makers is that facilities that might increase participation and study opportunities for women are seldom prioritised, particularly in terms of provision that would make for family-friendly services. In addition, an emphasis on vocational and work-based education and training has tended to benefit men more that women partly because of women's predominance in part-time work where the majority are responsible for paying their own fees for learning (Tuckett and Sargant, 1999).

Not only is participation in education gendered but also the subjects studied reflect a male/female dichotomy. This compartmentalisation results in some kinds of knowledge being considered more important and this is communicated very effectively in schools and other institutions. Subject specialisation, therefore, reinforces gender distinctions. In addition, an emphasis on new technologies as a way of advancing learning opportunities risks exacerbating social and gender divisions resulting in a 'society divided between the information-rich and the information-poor' (Fryer, 1997:21). Governments (DfEE, 1998; Scottish Office, 1998a) have put particular emphasis on the use of new technology to deliver learning. They have not shown, however, how the classed and gendered differences in access to, and familiarity with, these technologies are to be overcome (Engender, 1998). The gendered nature of participation in education and training is often ignored and instead 'equal opportunities' policies based on a meritocratic model are implemented. The meritocratic model ignores the process whereby opportunities are defined, interpreted and applied by those already in positions of power, which means that lifelong learning becomes one more way of reinforcing the status quo.

This means that a policy that is committed only to marginal changes will continue to preserve that world as it is. What is necessary is a 'problematising' approach (see Freire, 1972) that enables oppressed groups to reflect critically on their reality in a way that enables them to alter their social relations. In particular this should address the ways in which:

> Those who failed at school often come to see post-school learning of all kinds as irrelevant to their needs and capabilities. Hence not only is participation in further, higher and continuing education not perceived to

be a realistic possibility, but also work-based learning is viewed as unnecessary' (Rees et al, 1997: 1).

Education is not neutral and if people are treated first and foremost in relation to their potential contribution to the economy then a market value is attached to each individual according to that contribution. Rather than education becoming an individual and social force for emancipation it becomes instead an 'investment' on the part of employers and government.

Conclusion

This chapter has suggested that the lifelong learning policies present a powerful steer about what should be prioritised precisely because they are so all encompassing. However, by deconstructing these policies it is possible to identify a number of paradoxes that throw up contradictions which in turn create spaces for challenge and alternative action. The possibility of adults constructing their own knowledge and contesting their exclusion is not on the agenda of these policies but is a clear possibility for community educators wishing to engage in dialogues with excluded communities. Knowledge, skills, understanding, curiosity and wisdom cannot be kept in separate boxes, depending simply on who is paying for or providing them. This means that, although much of the funding that is tied to lifelong learning policy implementation is linked to programmes that focus on increasing people's employability, there are still spaces for action. Rather than a narrow conception of learning for the world of work the priority would be learning for citizenship leading to a revitalised sense of democratic and social purpose.

The idea of lifelong learning has not so far provoked much enthusiasm amongst the potential recipients of its intended benefits, especially those who know from their own lived experience that education has failed to make a quantitative difference to their lives in the past. They will need a lot of persuading that lifelong learning will be any different. As Jane Thompson (2001: 11) argues:

> The big challenge facing politicians and practitioners in these circumstances is to demonstrate the relevance and commitment of lifelong learning to tackling the urgent problems and real concerns of people living in the kind of difficult circumstances that would defeat the most courageous of us.

The next chapter considers a conception of the learning society that would contribute to a more inclusive democracy. It will discuss how community education practice can be constructed that focuses on the renewal of democracy, citizenship and social justice, rather than only the needs of the economy.

CHAPTER 3

LIFELONG LEARNING, KNOWLEDGE AND THE CURRICULUM

The real point, the real practicality [of education], was learning how to change your life. Really useful knowledge is knowledge calculated to make you free (Johnson, 1988: 21–22)

Introduction
One way in which lifelong learning could contribute to greater social inclusion is through an approach to knowledge and the development of the curriculum that starts from the issues and concerns of people rather than from externally imposed outcomes. This is because such learning involves the active engagement by citizens 'in the construction, interpretation, and, often, the re-shaping of their own social identity and social reality' (Cullen, 2001: 64). The engagement of people in creating their own knowledge involves developing a capacity for self determination and emphasises the social embeddedness of learning rather than its individual focus. The choices people make once they have had the opportunity to engage in dialogue about the focus of their learning are more open and are no longer limited by what providers wish to offer. These choices could be about the acquisition of vocational skills or qualifications but are equally likely to be about fulfilling social or cultural objectives. Such an approach to knowledge recognises that learning is located in social participation and dialogue as well as in the heads of individuals and treats 'teaching and learning not as two distinct activities, but as elements of a single, reciprocal process' (Coffield, 1999: 493).

In chapter two it was suggested that the deconstruction of lifelong learning policies allowed questions to be asked that were hidden from view. For example, currently employers exhort governments to provide the funding and structures that would enhance education and training provision so that they can benefit from a more skilled work force. An alternative approach would be to ask employers 'what value is the corporation to the community, how does it serve civic interests rather than just its own ledger of profit and loss' (Sennett, 1998: 137). Similarly, rather than seeing the purpose of engaging people in learning as primarily about serving the needs of the economy, the focus would instead be on learning that would increase democratic decision-making and active citizenship. The implications for lifelong learning that leads to democratic renewal are that community educators need to think about what would be 'really useful knowledge' to the people with whom they are working. Such knowledge is not value-free, but needs to seek out 'meaningful, practical starting points for curriculum negotiation within a critical structural analysis' (Johnston, 2000: 16). People, at whatever stage of their lives, would be empowered to make informed choices about what they wanted to learn based on an understanding of the opportunities and constraints affecting them. Moreover, this curriculum would be constructed from the intellectual and personal resources that people bring so that learning is about 'making knowledge that makes sense of their world' (Martin, 2001b: 4) and taking action that leads to change.

The remainder of this chapter provides an example of how community educators have worked with people from a socio-economically-excluded community to build knowledge and a curriculum that reflects their issues and concerns. The focus is on a family literacy project partly because of the importance that is attached in policy documents to the link between unemployment and literacy and basic skills difficulties. For example, the Scottish Executive (2001: 7) suggests 'in an increasingly globalised economy, Scotland's future prosperity depends on building up the skills of her existing workforce and improving the employability of those seeking work'. These concerns also emphasise the association of lifelong learning with skills, individual motivation and economic survival. Individualistic curricula reinforce the view that failure to learn is the fault of the individual, so it is important to provide an alternative perspective based on a sense of social purpose that is grounded in real lives and real learning practices. It is hoped that the emphasis on how people *use* literacy rather than why other people think they *need* these skills will demonstrate the importance of collaboratively constructing the curriculum of lifelong learning.

Current policy from the Scottish Executive with regard to literacy is rather contradictory and so it does provide opportunities for social purpose learning. This is because some of the problems associated with a deficit approach to learning have been recognised and, instead, a 'lifelong learning approach' is advocated. This approach:

> Rather than focusing on a minimum standard, is concerned more with establishing what the learner's goals are.... The aim is to access learners' ability to apply their learning to real contexts and to measure the economic, personal and social gains that they make, including their willingness to learn in the future (Scottish Executive, 2001: 14).

Such policies provide opportunities for community educators to ground literacy programmes in the life situations of adults and communities in response to issues that are derived from their own knowledge. It thus provides an alternative model of lifelong learning that contributes towards a more socially just society.

Family literacy
The common way to think about literacy is to see it as a ladder that people have to climb up. This ladder begins at school and the literacy that adults need is seen as the extension of this process in post-school contexts. The emphasis is,

therefore, on standardising literacy accomplishments through the use of tests, defining what are core skills, and pre-specifying uniform learning outcomes. People are ranked from bottom to top with the emphasis on what they can't do rather than what they can. This leads to a deficit model where those on the bottom rungs are positioned as lacking the skills that they need. The frameworks used to define this ladder are top-down ones, constructed largely in terms of pre-vocational and vocationally relevant literacy requirements. Consequently, they do not recognise the validity of people's own definitions, uses and aspirations for literacy, with the result that they are 'disempowering' in the sense that they are not negotiable or learner-centred and not locally responsive. They define what counts as 'real literacy' and silence everything else. If, however, the emphasis is put on how adults can and want to use literacy then the focus moves to what people have, rather than what they lack, what motivates them rather than what is seen as something they need (see Crowther et al, 2001: 2).

Family literacy programmes date from the mid-eighties, and identify the family as a whole as the site for educational intervention. The classification of these programmes as 'family literacy' arises from this wider focus, and the central element that these programmes have in common is consideration of the family as a 'learning unit'. Their central assumption is that the high degree of correlation between the literacy difficulties of the child and those of the parent means that these two areas of difficulty should be tackled together. One issue that such programmes are designed to address is the situation whereby teachers make assumptions about building upon home literacy experiences but have little idea of what actually happens in the home. This means that the literacy history of parents or the differences between home and community practices and those of the school are unexamined.

If the range of literacy activities that people already engage in and feel comfortable about can be built on then this is one way in which the culture of the home can be positively valued rather than being seen as an inadequate environment for the child's literacy development. How this might be done is illustrated by a family literacy project based in an outer-city housing estate in a poor working-class area of a Scottish city (see Haywood, 2000; Tett and Crowther, 1998). By taking a responsive approach to curriculum building — while at the same time positively valuing the home and community life of participants — it sought to include the literacy practices of everyday life in the curriculum and build on them. The participants in the project were parents of children who attended the primary schools in the area who had identified themselves as having literacy problems that they would like to work on in order to help themselves and their children. Groups of up to ten, of whom the vast majority were mothers, engaged in an educational programme that is detailed below.

Developing the curriculum
When they began the programme participants were asked to identify the literacy practices that they used in the home and community. 'Literacy' was widely

defined and included the ability to read, write and use numeracy, to handle information, to express ideas and opinions, to make decisions and solve problems (see Haywood, 2000). It was found that, although the programme participants regularly used a wide range of numeracy, reading and writing practices, they considered them unimportant. Everyday uses included: working out time tables and schedules; budgeting; scanning the TV pages to find out what was on; checking on their horoscopes; understanding a range of signs and symbols in the local environment; writing brief notes for family members; making shopping lists; keeping a note of birthdays and anniversaries; sending greetings cards. Recognising the importance of these literacy practices and working on them provided an appropriate starting point for the curriculum. This approach based education in everyday literacy concerns and practices and built on what people already knew and did, rather than emphasising what they could not do. It was coupled with a curriculum based on the students' concerns and aspirations about their own and their children's learning and relationships to their teachers. Combining this range of approaches provided a real incentive for learning because it concentrated on what really mattered to the participants.

Negotiating work in this way was not, however, simply a matter of passing responsibility for developing the curriculum from the tutor to the student; that would be an abdication of their critical, interpretative role. Tutors remained responsible for organising a pedagogical context where participants could collectively realise their best potential, where they all become subjects reflecting together *on* the process rather than passive individualised objects *of* the process. The project tutors were also committed to a particular understanding of their practice. One example was the valuing of home and community literacies and the fostering of effective understanding between home and school literacy practices. So was the way they emphasised the wealth of the knowledge that parents contribute to the educational development of their children.

Curriculum approaches were developed that built on a range of strategies that supported, rather than undermined, what parents did. For example, the project staff explicitly encouraged adults to think critically about their own school experiences and worked to avoid simplistic, pathological explanations of failure at school. In order to help participants think critically about these experiences they were asked to share their most positive and negative school learning episodes, which enabled the wide range of experience in the group to be discussed. This was coupled with student-led presentations that included reflecting upon their own experiences of school in ways that problematised their earlier internalised understandings of failure. In addition, they were asked to discuss the differences between their own school experiences and those of their children in order to identify changing pedagogical practices. Similarly, participants were encouraged to identify and value their own educative role with their children. This included teaching their children local songs and games as well as talking about daily events. The emphasis was on the positive ways in which parents already successfully educated their children through different ways of knowing the world instead of assuming that parents lacked knowledge and skills that the teacher had to impart (see Taylor and Dorsey-Gaines, 1988).

Using the literacy practices of everyday life
This project also sought to include the literacy practices of everyday life in the curriculum so that the home and community life of participants was positively valued. Students kept a log of their own reading and writing practices and also interviewed others about their role as readers and writers in the family. A significant range of oral communication, reading and writing practices were revealed which people regularly engaged in but were considered insignificant. These included adult-child conversations that, as Tizard and Hughes (1984:9) have pointed out, are rich learning experiences. Recognising and working on actual literacy practices provided an appropriate starting point for the curriculum because it grounded educational intervention in the problems of everyday life. This included challenging assumptions about the homogeneity of reading and writing practices since the wide variation in the group's experiences and the influence of gender, ethnicity and class on what was considered 'normal' was revealed through their discussions. Critical examination of the presumptions about family life that were contained in their children's reading books revealed assumptions about nuclear family roles that were at odds with many of the participants' own experiences. The next stage of this part of the project was for the participants to create, with the help of the computers, stories for their children that reflected their own lives. Access to good word-processing and drawing packages enabled attractive texts to be produced which were authentic reflections of the relevant issues in their own families and communities.

The project staff also focused on developing critical language awareness through enabling learners to see language and the reading of texts as problematic (see Wallace, 1992). This involved, for example, collecting texts that the participants came across in everyday use from a range of genres (advertisements, newspapers, letters from school, bills, cereal packets, 'junk mail', and family photograph albums) to work on as a group. They were asked to identify: to whom the text was primarily addressed; who produced it; why it was interesting and what message the producer was trying to get across so that they could see that all writing was created for a particular purpose. Such decoding challenged the participants' taken-for-granted assumptions that there was just one form of writing and helped them to see that the writing that they created could vary in form too. Student-led investigations, which involved taking polaroid photographs of a range of public writing including graffiti, public notices, shop signs, posters, and then coming together to decode these pictures, enabled discussion to take place about the concerns in the community and the messages that were presented to them. Both these approaches enabled the participants to see the ways in which literacy is constructed in different contexts and for different purposes and led to lively discussions. Two examples were the prevalence of racism in the community as revealed through graffiti on the walls of the houses and how particular family life-styles, including having two parents, were assumed by the manufacturers of breakfast cereals.

Sometimes the materials produced by the students were used to create a group poem around the theme of the discussion so that individual contributions led to a collective, co-operative outcome. On other occasions, the theme generated letters of complaint to the appropriate authorities, for example, in relation to the removal of racist graffiti. The general approach of the project was to link reading with writing and talking so that these three important facets of literacy could be brought together into a seamless web. Oral language was regarded as important especially in relation to rhymes, story-telling and word games and was used to highlight the importance of using the language of the home and community in other contexts including the school.

Another important aspect of the project was the use of authentic assessment situated in real life contexts, which is done *with*, not *to*, participants. The ability to make changes in their practices and take action was used to assess their progress rather than standardised tests. This process oriented focus involved students developing a 'portfolio' of examples of their literacy work as evidence of what they had learnt. Portfolios included the titles of books that participants had read with their children, stories that they had created about their own family life, letters written to friends and families, diaries, examples of reading and writing from a variety of contexts including church, neighbourhood meetings, work as well as photographs of writing that had interested them. This type of assessment helped the students to reflect both on what they had learned and also how they learned and gave them opportunities to test out their newly acquired skills. Reflection was enhanced when the portfolio was brought along to the group and formed part of a 'show and tell' session which could also be shared with the children. Assessment was based on the extent to which students had been able to change their literacy practices from their own baselines. This type of assessment also allowed changes in relationships, particularly with their children and the school, to be recorded. This was a very different approach from the way in which people's learning is normally assessed, through the use of standardised outcome-based methods, and was empowering to both learners and tutors. For learners it enabled them to take responsibility for their own learning and have an equal say in the direction it should take. For tutors it provided feedback on the programme design, content and delivery and the strengths and weaknesses of their approaches.

By taking a problematising approach to speaking, reading and writing practices the participants in this project were enabled to see that there are a variety of literacies rather than just the one used by the school. This, in turn, helped to challenge the deficit views of the culture of the home and the community that had been internalised by parents. As they gained confidence in their own literacy practices they were able to interact on a more equal basis with the school's staff so that they were involved more directly in their children's education. This required the development of a greater understanding by teachers of what parents needed to know about school practices that was partly achieved through joint training sessions with the family literacy project and school staff. The other aspect of confidence-building was through helping parents be in a better position to know what to ask the school about their children's progress that took account of the culture of the local community. Parents learnt by sharing and valuing experiences as well as by suggestions and ideas introduced by the tutor. So the project subtly aided the process of generating new knowledge based on the local culture by making the implicit pedagogical activities of the parents explicit.

Emphasising strengths
This family literacy project made a useful contribution to shifting the way that the literacy 'problem' has been defined. The curriculum developed involved the recognition that some people are at a disadvantage because of the ways in which a particular literacy is used in dominant institutions. 'The culture children learn as they grow up is, in fact, "ways of taking" meaning from the environment around them' (Heath, 1983: 49) and not a 'natural' way of behaving. The social practices of the school and other institutions, and the language and literacy they reinforce, need to be made visible to show that they represent a selection from a wider range of possibilities, none of which is neutral. These practices then become a critical resource for learning and literacy. An important issue here was the use of Scots for everyday language and literacy. As the Scottish Consultative Council on the Curriculum (1996:15) has pointed out, since Scots is the language of the home for many people, it provides speakers with their first awareness of themselves and their relationships. Use of the language also helps people to:

> Establish their own sense of values, and [is] closely involved in the development of thinking skills, and those related, equally important, worlds of feeling and social consciousness. Neglecting Scots has, therefore, unwelcome social and personal consequences.

An important 'unwelcome consequence' that is easily internalised is that the language of people's homes and communities is only of value within a very limited range of social contexts. An investigation carried out by Alan Addison in relation to this issue asked adult literacy students 'Dae ye speak Scots or slang?' (Do you speak Scots or do you use slang) and nearly 70% of the students responded 'I speak slang'. He points out, 'if a community's means of communication and self expression are perceived by themselves to be inferior how then does that reflect on their self-image and confidence' (Addison, 2001: 156)? If the language and literacy of the home and community is unacknowledged or actively suppressed then it becomes difficult for people to say what is important to them in ways that are meaningful. People become voiceless by not being allowed to speak, or only being allowed to say what has already been said by others and so they eventually learn how to silence themselves. As long as people remain voiceless with their own lived experience interpreted on their behalf by others then their own meanings are rendered illegitimate and disqualified. Henry Giroux (1992: 170) has argued that people need to be able 'to reclaim their own memories, stories and histories as part of an on-going collective struggle to challenge those power structures that attempt to silence them'.

Community educators could play a part in this struggle through a clear and proactive commitment to emphasising the wealth of people's knowledge rather than their deficits. This involves valuing difference and building a curriculum that starts from people's everyday uses, meanings and purposes for reading and writing and developing authentic texts which reflect the reality of their lives. It also requires access to, and use of, the resources available in the home and the community to support these practices. Community educators also need to recognise that 'personal troubles' are 'public issues' (Mills, 1959) and so ensure that all public knowledge and public agendas are subjected to critical questioning in ways that challenge the prevailing 'common sense'. This, in turn, leads to the development of literacies that are about people writing their own stories that reflect their own lives, rather than only reading other peoples' books to their children.

Linking formal and informal learning
This project was also an important reminder of the value of using the informal learning, developed and controlled by the group, to create a curriculum using their own ideas. The value of informal learning, where people attach meaning and significance to shared experiences and common understandings with others, is an important corrective to the assumption that learning is little other than a marketable commodity to be dispensed by others. Informal learning provides a reminder that learners have social agency that enables them to engage in the dynamic process of making sense of complicated lives in a variety of contexts and circumstances. By linking this kind of learning into more formal contexts people can make sense of some of this experience and add new and different knowledge. Recognising the relationship between informal and formal learning puts learners back at the heart of learning, as the subjects of learning rather than the objects of educational interventions that are supposed to be good for them. If learners are positioned as experienced and knowledgeable social actors then they become active players rather than passive recipients of education. Learning then becomes a shared endeavour between tutors and students, a two-way, rather than a one-way, process (see Thompson, 2001).

An alternative discourse of lifelong learning
What counts as important knowledge in relation to literacy, access to information and effective communication skills all need to be considered as part of the way inequalities of power are systematically reproduced. In a democracy, political representatives, public institutions and services, the activities of those who work for them (e.g. doctors, teachers, welfare workers), community organisations and groups, have to be accountable to the people they represent, or work for, if democracy is to become a way of life. Literacy education should, therefore, contribute towards enabling people to interrogate the claims and activities done on their behalf and, in turn, encourage them to develop the skill, analysis and confidence to make their own voice heard (Crowther and Tett, 2001: 109). Education should also help people to engage in a wide range of political roles and social relationships that occur outside both the workplace and the marketplace.

Community educators need, through their daily practice, to demonstrate the efficacy of this model of lifelong learning that focuses on learning for democratic renewal rather than on increasing economic competitiveness. Seeing the effects of this way of working in action helps policy makers, and others involved in the delivery of education and training, to understand that alternative constructs for learning are effective in enabling individuals and communities to fulfil their social and personal, as well as their economic, needs. The diverse purposes and contradictions of lifelong learning highlighted in chapter two provides challenges and opportunities for community educators and places them in a central position to debate the ideas and how they might be interpreted. This is a position that they should be exploiting, since the ambiguity of policies provides opportunities to use these spaces to develop a more radical practice. Lifelong learning policies can also offer opportunities for the fostering of active citizenship and social inclusion. For example, the Scottish Executive suggests that 'an inclusive society is also a literate society' (2001: 8). Stimulating and supporting lifelong learning for a more active and inclusive construction of citizenship involves marginalised people recognising that their capacity for learning and generating new knowledge is their key resource.

Lifelong learning and the opportunities it represents can be used as a unifying force, not only between providers but also between different interest groups, in ways that ensure that this process challenges oppression and exclusion. This will involve the nurturing of an education and training system whose function is not to reflect and reproduce existing inequalities in society but rather one that prioritises provision for those whose earlier educational and socio-economic disadvantage would give them a first claim in a genuinely lifelong learning system. Educators can then act as an emancipatory force for change especially if they start:

> From the problems, experiences and social position of excluded majorities, from the position of the working people, women and black people. It means working up these lived experiences and insights until they fashion a real alternative (Johnson, 1988: 813).

Within this paradigm people's classed and gendered experiences would be seen as a learning resource to be used, rather than a deficiency to be rectified.

Conclusion
This chapter has demonstrated the importance of learning that builds on experience and emphasises the wealth of people's knowledge rather than their deficits. This approach requires the joint development of a curriculum based on the valuing of the knowledge that people bring from their own family and community contexts. The curriculum also needs to enable the development of a critical understanding of the social, political and economic factors that shape experience. Building knowledge and a curriculum that reflects the issues and concerns of ordinary people is an empowering process that does lead to 'really useful knowledge' and an alternative discourse of lifelong learning. Radical

community educators have a role to act as 'agents of social justice and as crucial resources in the struggles of ordinary people for a fuller sense of democratic and inclusive citizenship' (Martin, 2001b: 6). This is a difficult task but vital if lifelong learning policies can be used to contribute to the struggle to bring about 'democracy as a way of life' (ibid.). The challenge is to capture the positive and enthusiastic belief in the power of learning and in the potential of all people that comes from engaging in more democratic decision-making about what is important knowledge in the construction of the curriculum. This type of learning society, that has at its heart the qualities of 'co-operating in the practice of change and critically reviewing it' (Ranson, 1998:28), would provide some real choices about what being a citizen means and show how everyone can contribute to democratic processes. A 'whole life — all life' approach would place the learner's needs and experience at the centre and help people to engage in the wide range of political roles and social relationships that occur outside both the workplace and the marketplace.

The next chapter will discuss how some of the issues highlighted through these approaches to lifelong learning, knowledge and the curriculum can contribute to social inclusion and the building of a more equal society.

CHAPTER 4

SOCIAL EXCLUSION AND LIFELONG LEARNING

The excluded do not constitute a defined group in the population: there is no single clear-cut definition of 'social exclusion'. Categories such as the 'unskilled' 'ethnic minorities' 'the unemployed' cover a range of circumstances.... So 'exclusion' does not bring a precise target into view but a range of associated issues (OECD, 1999: 15–16).

Introduction
'Social exclusion', like lifelong learning, has been subjected to many interpretations. Generally the term has been associated with the long established and deep-rooted problems of poverty and unemployment that have been exacerbated by growing social and economic inequalities. In response to these problems the stated aim of social inclusion policies is to ensure that all citizens, whatever their social or economic background, have opportunities to participate fully in society and enjoy a high quality of life. It is argued that education and lifelong learning have a central role to play in this process since they have the potential to 'change people's lives, even transform them' (Fryer, 1997: 24) and give them an economic and political voice through participation in the labour market and enhanced citizenship.

John Field has argued that the use of the term 'social exclusion' throughout Western Europe reflects a policy change. He suggests that 'rather than struggling against the social causes of inequality, the new language of exclusion implies that government's task is to promote "inclusion" into the existing social order' (Field, 2000: 108). The link between lifelong learning and social exclusion, from this perspective, is that programmes to combat social exclusion centre on the rectification of personal deficits through training and are founded on the notion that people must acquire the skills that the labour market needs of them. Another link lies in the view that extremes of inequality can be economically damaging and provide a risk to social cohesion because people become disengaged from society if they are not stakeholders in the economy. The answer then is to enable people to gain employment so that they are taken out of poverty and actively engaged in society.

Along with the de-emphasising of socio-economic inequality and the concern for wealth redistribution have been different ideas about how inequalities are viewed. There has been a waning sense of the social obligation of the 'haves' to the 'have nots', which means that the old appeals to duty and the responsibility of society to its less fortunate members have fallen on deaf ears. For example, the British Social Attitudes Survey, reported on in November 2001, found that attitudes to the poor had hardened.

> In 1994, 15 per cent attributed the plight of the poor to "laziness or lack of will power"; in 2000, this had risen to 23 per cent. Conversely, in 1994, 30 per cent blamed poverty on "injustice in our society"; in 2000, this had dropped to 21 per cent (New Statesman, 2001: 6).

This shift in attitudes, at its most extreme, can become a fear of the excluded themselves. This group have been described by some commentators as becoming an underclass who have effectively dropped out of society and live from a mixture of crime and welfare benefits. Given these attitudes then appeals for greater spending to alleviate poverty are couched in terms of assuaging middle class fears of the poor and as an investment, rather than a gift. Thus the Liberal Democrat Party's *'Commission on wealth creation and social cohesion'* warned that:

> Exclusion is the greatest risk accompanying the opportunities of the new economic era. Significant numbers of people lose their hold on the labour market, then on the social and political participation in their community. An underclass emerges, consisting of people who live their separate lives often characterised by a combination of destitution, dependence on welfare payments and other benefits, occasional windfalls, crime, and apathy (Dahrendorf, 1995: 15).

This leads to the argument that social inclusion is best promoted through a commitment to lifelong learning and this commitment is becoming used as a marker of whether a community is likely to prove a worthwhile investment for the future by both private and public sector organisations. The difficulty here is that lifelong learning has an overwhelmingly positive image. Not participating in it can mean that marginalised people are likely to accept their exclusion as the (just) reward for their own failure to participate. This discourse then gets internalised by individuals in ways that are profoundly damaging to their own sense of worth and value.

Are there alternative possibilities to this discourse? What is clearly missing is the recognition that low wages, insecure employment, and dependence on means-tested benefits all contribute to social exclusion. Income inequality matters in any consideration of social exclusion because 'income is both the basis of social participation through consumption and a reflection of the power of people in their economic roles' (Byrne, 1999: 79). From this viewpoint social exclusion is an active process that is about exclusion from power as well as material assets. As Madanipour and colleagues (1998: 22) point out

> Social exclusion is… a multi-dimensional process, in which various forms of exclusion are combined: participation in decision making and political processes, access to employment and material resources, and integration into common cultural processes. When combined they create acute forms of exclusion that find a spatial manifestation in particular neighbourhoods.

This means that social exclusion can only be understood as a relational term that is really about the social processes that reproduce inequalities of power and resources, reinforce low self-esteem, undermine status and lower expectations. Combating social exclusion and increasing participation thus requires redistributive measures as well as enabling the needs and interests of marginalised communities to be articulated and acted on. It also has to be on people's own terms, where they are seen as actively contributing to their communities rather than passively receiving 'hand outs' from society.

How the problem of social exclusion is conceived leads to different solutions. If the problem is seen in terms of a discourse of individual responsibility and pathology then the solution lies in changing these individuals. If, on the other hand, it is recognised that social exclusion is a structural issue that arises from the fundamentally unequal nature of society then the solution is conceived differently. Social inclusion thus requires the recognition that the people living in excluded communities are not the problem, rather they are the solution. People have agency and their actions can make a difference to their conditions.

There are opportunities for community educators to use the spaces created by these policy ambiguities to create more inclusive action for change. This is helped by the recognition of the Social Justice Department of the Scottish Executive that social exclusion is a relational term that derives from inequality.

> Some communities and groups face concentrations of deprivation and exclusion, sometimes as a result of structural inequalities and labour market effects, and sometimes due to discrimination and inequality. Building strong, thriving communities is central to our... strategy. We need to work together to plan for greater inclusion and to support communities to... take ownership of their own futures (Scottish Executive, 2000b: 4).

In order to illustrate the possibilities for community educators this chapter will examine two projects, one working with young people and the other with adults. Both projects have attempted to help build more inclusive approaches to inequalities through educational interventions that have led to an increase in collective action for change.

Young people and social exclusion
Young people who come from socio-economically-disadvantaged backgrounds can be particularly subject to social exclusion and two main factors contribute to this. One is their very low income and the other is their absence of 'voice' and both reflect their lack of power to make decisions that effect their lives. In terms of income inequality, young people who come from disadvantaged backgrounds and who leave school with few educational qualifications have borne the brunt of industrial change, with large numbers facing the prospect of unemployment and movement from one training scheme to another. This experience is inter-generational since young people who come from families where other members are unemployed are more than twice as likely to face

long-term unemployment as those from families with no unemployment (Cartmel, 2000). As Fred Cartmel points out:

> Government training schemes are based on a deficiency model whereby the young person lacks the basic skills to advance into employment; but in Scotland the social structure is to blame for the majority of young people's unemployment, especially in Glasgow where there are no jobs (2000: 32).

Many commentators have characterised this group of excluded young people as seeking to avoid work and as threatening the established order. Research has shown, however, that they see work as very important because it is 'a key source of self-respect, the principle definer of personal identity and a social duty' (MacDonald, 1997: 195). However, the link between work and education is not clear to them and so a low value is often placed on education, with priority being given to getting a 'proper job'. Young people can also display apathy towards politics and the political system. This is partly caused by a lack of political culture and understanding that is derived from their being excluded from any contact with politics through the school curriculum until very recently (Brynner, 2001). These attitudes, coupled with the inadequacy of the social support that young people receive in making transitions from school to work and from parental home to independence, lead to difficulties in engaging with young people in ways that are responsive to their needs.

Current debates about young people tend to focus on their deficiencies and lack of responsibility rather than their marginality or the impact of structural inequalities on their lives. Little value is placed on their views, aspirations and analyses of their situations with the result that young people rightly view society as treating them unjustly as they continue to have messages about their lack of worth reinforced. Without a commitment to engagement and participation of marginalised young people they will be perceived only as a problem with their voices excluded from the debate. Accepting that young people have specific rights reduces their dependence on adults to provide, protect and speak for them and hence their individual and collective vulnerability is lessened. A clear commitment to practices that recognise young people as active participants, rather than passive consumers, can reduce their exclusion from society.

Giving young people a voice
In most major cities there are young people who have been pushed out to the edges of society where they are effectively excluded from participating in the communities in which they live. These young people lead a lifestyle that may place them at risk through drug use, crime (both as victim and perpetrator) and prostitution and, although they may live at home, to all intents and purposes they mostly live out on the streets. It is common for young people to avoid contact with adults who represent authority to them such as teachers, social workers and police. These young people face a range of socio-economic problems that include inadequate housing, worklessness and poor health. As

was suggested earlier many of the solutions to social exclusion are premised on the social integration of economically marginal groups through the gaining of educational qualifications and paid work. This is regarded as particularly important for young people who are seen as threatening the established order. It is also premised on a deficit approach that assumes that young people have nothing to offer or to say about the factors that would make a difference to their lives.

In order to consider the possibilities for community educators this case study draws on the work of Ken McCulloch (2000: 41–44) and the Edinburgh Street-work Project (ESP). ESP has been in operation since 1991 as a detached youth work project working with young people mainly in the streets of the city centre but also in peripheral areas. Detached youth workers operate by engaging young people in conversation in their space, on pavements or park benches, and listening carefully to what they have to say. These workers recount how often young people will talk with remarkable frankness about their hopes and worries, about their families and relationships, about sex and drugs, about their physical and emotional health and life in general. In turn, youth workers can provide information and advice about safe sex practices, about hostel accommodation, about legal rights and responsibilities, depending on the young person's own interests. The emphasis of the work is actively to encourage young people to assess risk-taking and law-breaking, for example in relation to proscribed drugs, for themselves By using young people's own experiences as a starting point and taking their views seriously they can be encouraged to take their own thought-through decisions. In this way young people are enabled to make more informed choices, to appreciate the consequences of their actions, and to value themselves, their bodies and other people. Workers seek to grasp these moments, to explore topics, to provide good information, and to encourage young people's exploration of the issues that effect them.

Many of the young people who were contacted by ESP were very conscious of their place in society and were aware that they were seen as a nuisance by other people. They were also quick to point out that they were 'hanging about' because they had nowhere else to go. Their argument was that their lack of money and suitable, affordable, local resources meant that they could not fully participate in the life of their community. As a result of interventions on the street by workers a group of young people came together from five different housing estates in Edinburgh to take action about the issues that were important to them. They wrote to their local councillors, the manager of the local Social Inclusion Partnership and their MSP about the lack of services in their area. As a result they were invited to a meeting that enabled them to learn about the proposed regeneration of their area. The young people grasped this opportunity to put forward their ideas for resources and services that they argued should be included in any redevelopment plans. The main areas that they argued for included the setting up a youth café and better access to existing facilities.

These may appear to be small gains and there are still many problems for this group, who have been perceived as difficult and uncooperative, to overcome.

One of these problems includes the hostility of many of the people who have responsibilities for more co-operative and settled young people. What has been achieved, however, is that this group of young people has participated in decision-making in their own communities and had their voices heard. Their views may not have been very welcome because they were asking for changes to be made and in a manner that was often confrontational and dissented from plans already agreed with the more 'respectable' members of the community.

The work of ESP demonstrates the possibility of youth work that values young people's rights to protest and dissent. It is an example of practice that supports young people to have a voice in decisions that effect their everyday lives. This approach promotes inclusion and citizenship through the encouragement of young people's rights to campaign and protest. It is concerned to enable voices to be heard that, in the established order, are often ignored or even suppressed. It provides an alternative to the common prescriptions for the social inclusion of young people that prioritises the gaining of educational qualifications and entry into paid work. Once young people's agency in making decisions is emphasised a different understanding of the solutions to social exclusion is possible that sees them as active subjects, rather than passive victims. This project has achieved some limited, but nonetheless useful, reforms. What has not been tackled, however, are the structural inequalities that ultimately have the strongest impact on their life chances.

Social exclusion and health
Another factor that contributes to social exclusion is health, an area in which Scotland's population lags behind many of its European partners. A great deal of research has shown how poor health is linked to inequality, poverty and social class both in terms of the diseases people die from and the illness they suffer (Acheson, 1998; Scottish Executive Health Department, 2001). For example, a baby whose father is an unskilled manual worker is one and a half times more likely to die before the age of one than the baby of a manager. In addition, the poorest children are twice as likely to die from respiratory illnesses and more than four times as likely to be killed in a road traffic accident as those from social class I (Leon et al, 1992). As Graham, (2000: 90) puts it, 'Social class is written on the body: it is inscribed in our experiences of health and our chances of premature death'. Similarly people's experience of the place where they live is also fundamental to the quality and meaning of their day-to-day life and health. These include social relations with people, the physical fabric of the locality and the local geographies of services and facilities. Research demonstrates that, in combination, features of place can be either sustaining or undermining of psychosocial well-being and health (Gattrell et al, 2000: 166).

This large-scale research can be put into a local context by examining the impact of a course called 'Health Issues in the Community'. The course has involved people from a range of socio-economically excluded areas and groups throughout Scotland in investigating their concerns about local health issues. The course has provided opportunities for people to express their own views, and to question everyday assumptions and explanations, particularly where they differ from their own experience. It draws on people's lived experience of individual and community health problems to build a curriculum based on the issues that are important to them and their communities. This has involved tutors developing a meaningful relationship with each group so that the design of the programme takes account of the influences that impact on them. Like the literacy project described in the previous chapter it considers the role that learning can play in challenging social exclusion and the role of the participants' own knowledge in contributing to change.

The assumption underpinning the course is that damaging social experiences produce ill-health and that remedial action needs to be social. This view of health focuses on the socio-economic risk conditions such as poverty, unemployment, pollution, poor housing and power imbalances that cause ill-health. It also emphasises that 'people's experiences of health are more about the quality of their emotional and social situation than about their experience of disease or disability' (Labonte, 1997: 9). The perspective taken by the course is that an important way that inequalities in health can be tackled, and social exclusion reduced, is to find ways of strengthening individuals and communities so that they can join together for mutual support. As Whitehead (1995: 25) points out, 'research shows that by people joining together you can strengthen the whole community's defence against health hazards'.

At the end of each course participants investigate and write about a health issue in their community that they believe is important and a selection of their writings has been published in three books edited by Jane Jones (1999a & b, 2001). This chapter draws on these published writings by using the words of the participants to demonstrate the impact of these health issues and the action they took to bring about change. The names of the students are pseudonyms

Housing and Health

Poor housing is one of the major health issues identified by those living in socio-economically-excluded communities. As one student put it:

> In my community due to poor housing design and inadequate heating systems families are forced to live with dampness. If they did heat their houses properly they probably would not be able to afford to eat, and are therefore forced to live with dampness in their homes (Frank, in Jones, 1999b: 8).

High-rise flats are a common feature of socially excluded communities and the isolation this type of housing causes, is another factor that leads to stress and depression. 'Isolation is a major problem in the flats as you can go for days without seeing anybody' (Cathy, in Jones, 1999b: 9). Animosity between neighbours is also a problem when people are living, quite literally, on top of each other. This is often combined with overcrowding, especially for those with large or extended families.

Participants in the course demonstrated that one way of ending the spiral of despair regarding poor housing and ill health is through community development.

This means that rather than seeing dampness and the noise pollution caused by poor housing as an individual trouble, that must be solved by an individual taking action on his or her own, the reasons behind the problem are examined.

> The way forward is through the community development process where individuals come together and tackle the problem as a public issue rather than a private one. Their strategy then becomes forcing the housing department to address the problem of poor housing and developing effective procedures in dealing with noisy neighbours (Alan, in Jones, 1999b: 35).

Through the process of developing strategies for tackling the problems and taking their issues to the wider community a group can grow in confidence and eventually will be able to take well thought out solutions to policy-makers. One group involved in the course eventually gained better insulation, cladding, soundproofing and heating for their houses through a long campaign of local and wider action. As one member of the group suggested:

> The [better housing] had an instant effect on improving people's health both directly and indirectly by reducing people's stress and anxiety levels. Your home should be a place where you can relax, unwind and escape from the outside world (Jimmy, in Jones, 1999b: 35).

Contesting official definitions of health
It appears that the medical dominance over the definition and analysis of health and illness is still disproportionately influential in health policy and practice (see Carlisle, 2001; Graham, 2000; Purdy and Banks, 1999). It is still difficult for policy-makers to recognise the political and social determinants of health, and to make the connections between the psychosocial effects of lack of control over the social and material conditions of people's lives, and poor health. Moreover, there is a pervasive assumption that it is people's individual life styles that need to be changed in order to improve health rather than their social and material conditions. Contesting these official definitions of health was, therefore, a key issue in working with communities on their own health issues. This had a number of implications that are explored below.

If people feel that they are able to take action about their circumstances and recognise that their problems are not their individual responsibility then much can change. For example, one student was angry that the media blamed people for their own poverty and got together with other people to see what they could do. The group talked to community education staff and they helped them to sort out what were the important issues and how to work from there. She explained:

> Healthy diet was a big issue and it was the priority. The shopping centre was the only place in our town that you could get fresh fruit and vegetables but the prices were way above most people's budgets. We decided to take action first of all about telling people what were healthy foods. Then we

went to our local farmer to buy our fruit and vegetables so that we could sell them cheaper, only adding on the cost of petrol. The group sent out leaflets giving information on where to go to buy cheaper fruit and vegetables, the response was staggering. Everyone knows what a healthy diet is but they just can't afford it (Hetty, in Jones, 2001: 33).

A challenge for people is to see the potential that effective social action has in de-privatising their pain. Poor people often blame themselves for the burdens that they carry and hide their feelings of guilt and inadequacy away. One aspect of changing this is to challenge the stigma associated with mental health and the medical solutions that are offered. Participants in the course described their worries about going to the doctor with their symptoms and their fears about the impact this would have on their children. For example, one student said, 'It is really frightening to say what you feel. You think, if I tell them that, the bairns [children] will get taken away. You're frightened of being labelled a bad mother' (Joan, in Jones, 1999a: 91).

Moving from an individual solution to one that comes from collective action is the next step in the process of analysis but this usually needs the intervention of 'skilled helpers' (see Brookfield, 2000). One way in which the 'Health Issues in the Community' course provides such help is to show how apparently private troubles are actually public issues (Mills, 1959). An important aspect of this has been to look at the issue of mental health. For example, two students commented on the ways in which their own understanding had changed:

> I had been on tranquillisers but I felt so ashamed about it that I hid it from everyone. Then this young woman spoke up about her experience in the discussion group and I realised that lots of women had had the same feelings. You have to learn that it isn't your fault but you need people to talk to about it first (Laura, in Jones, 1999a: 130).

> I'm involved with the Stress Centre now that got set up because a group of us thought about what would have helped us more than just getting a prescription. We decided that it was somewhere to go to get some support and someone to talk to, so we met a lot of different people and eventually the Centre was set up. Working there has done a lot for my self-confidence and I know that we can help people. It takes time but it can be done (Norah, in Jones, 1999a: 133).

Working with a community to increase self-determination through collective organisation and action is an important task for educators. Building organisations, taking action to redistribute resources, ensuring that community voices are heard all have direct health benefits. This is because lack of control over one's own destiny promotes a susceptibility to ill-health for people who live in difficult situations where they do not have adequate resources or supports in their day-to-day lives (see Graham, 2000). Clearly the people who participated in this course have involved themselves in action that has enabled them to have their voices listened to about the issues about health that are important to them.

This has raised their self-esteem and confidence, and had some impact on decision-making and the use and distribution of resources in relation to health.

Learning, voice and social inclusion
The personal and social damage inflicted by inequality, social exclusion and restricted opportunity is immense. An important component of social inclusion is learning which should represent a resource for people to help them identify inequalities, probe their origins and begin to challenge them, using skills, information and knowledge in order to achieve and stimulate change. Through this type of learning, the production of knowledge is put back into the hands of people, competing values can be thought about and their relevance for people's lives can be assessed (see Fryer, 1997). Clearly, whilst learning alone cannot abolish inequality and social divisions it can make a limited but important contribution to combating them, not least by tackling the ways in which social exclusion is reinforced through the very processes and outcomes of education.

If people can be helped to challenge individually-based, deficit views of themselves and their communities then a small step has been taken in enabling their voices to be heard. Enabling communities to name and frame their problems for themselves and build their own 'really useful knowledge' (Johnson, 1988) thus becomes an important benefit of learning. Instead of emphasising disease and ill-health and individual's lifestyles as the problem the ways in which well-being can flourish can be redefined. Rather than seeing young people as a problem the solutions that they can offer to improve their own lives through having their voices heard can be advanced. As bell hooks (1989: 17) has suggested:

> Moving from silence into speech is for the oppressed... a gesture of defiance that heals, that makes new life and new growth possible. It is that act of speech, of 'talking back' that is no mere gesture of empty words, that is the expression of our movement from subject to object — the liberated voice.

A community development approach enables people to establish for themselves what their issues are and provides a means through which they can explore the root causes of their problems. The impact of such work can be seen in three broad areas. Firstly, it leads to an increase in agency and thus greater well-being through increased self-esteem and confidence. Secondly, there is more local influence over decision-making, thus potentially improving the provision of services to meet locally identified needs. Finally, a holistic approach to community capacity-building can contribute towards the creation of an alternative framework through which to understand local issues from a broad-based, sustainable perspective.

Conclusion
This chapter has examined the concept of social exclusion and shown how the dominant discourse of individual responsibility and pathology has contributed

to further marginalising those who are living in poverty. It has illustrated an alternative discourse that instead emphasises the role of those who are being excluded through two case studies. These projects have provided opportunities for people to express their own views, and to question everyday assumptions and definitions, particularly where they differed from their own experience. In a field where official definitions of social exclusion can exert a powerful influence the projects illustrated have sought to help local people focus on explanations that are meaningful to them because they come from their own experience. By taking action, for example over the stigmatisation involved in mental health issues or the lack of appropriate facilities, local people assume control and create, rather than receive, meaningful knowledge. Working together collectively and then taking action based on what has been learnt is an empowering process as people start to take back some control over their own destiny and directly improve their own communities. People then are no longer shut out from their rights as citizens in society but instead can use their knowledge to act purposefully to advance their collective interests.

These case studies have illustrated the importance of responding to the voices of those who are excluded. When people do not have their voices heard their only other option is to exit from participation in decision making to the detriment of the wider society which then creates policies *for* people rather than *with* them. As Ian Martin (1987:) argues:

> "Community education" is about evolving more open, participatory and democratic relationships between educators and their constituencies... . The reciprocal quality of these relationships is crucial: community educators claim to work with people — not for them, let alone on them... . This fundamental element of role redefinition and reversal has wide ranging implications for the nature of educative relationships, the context of learning and the potential for redistribution of educational opportunity.

Faced with a dominant discourse that blames people for the poverty that they suffer it is easy for these feelings of failure to be internalised and so confidence and self-esteem are lost. When people are excluded from participation in decision-making as well as access to employment and material resources then individual action that will change their circumstances becomes almost impossible. The development of local coalitions against exclusion such as those illustrated here, however, can lead to the development of a political culture that emphasises the fundamentally unequal nature of society rather than people's individual deficits. Emphasising the importance of the redistribution of resources shows that there are alternatives to increasing inequalities. These alternatives will grow out of the local politics that are founded in civil society. Popular participation in these more active forms of politics therefore needs to become central to the process of democratic renewal in Scotland (see Crowther, 1999). Community education cannot change society but it can be an important resource for communities struggling to change their circumstances. The next chapter will discuss some ways in which this might be done.

CHAPTER 5

COMMUNITY EDUCATION, RISK AND THE
EDUCATION OF DESIRE

Increasingly we feel comfortable with seeing people as victims of their own circumstances rather than authors of their own lives. The outcome of these developments is a world that equates the good life with self-limitation and risk aversion (Furedi, 1997: 147).

Introduction
A healthy democracy requires a robust civil society in which a variety of constituencies are capable of making their voices heard. Currently, however, whilst there is a great deal of rhetoric about the importance of empowering learners to be more autonomous, powerful socio-economic pressures make this increasingly difficult. One of these pressures is a pervasive pessimism that issues such as 'globalisation' are beyond our control and it is impossible to protect others and ourselves from its effects. As the above quotation reminds us, people are increasingly seen as victims of fate who cannot help themselves or work out their own responses to problems. In turn this creates an insidious dependence on experts to 'help' people deal with experiences 'appropriately' and this dependence can fuel mistrust of other sources of support such as peers, family and local communities. Belief in the power of fate, and doubts about people's ability to cope with life, undermine personal autonomy and responsibility whilst leading us to accept closer state regulation of behaviour (see Furedi, 1997: 150).

It seems important to challenge these discourses that constrain the capability of people to take control of their own learning otherwise compliance, rather than change, will be the result. This chapter seeks to examine whether community education can make a difference to people's lives through challenging these 'victim' discourses. It will consider strategies that can encourage people to take back control. One important consideration is how the ability of all citizens can be acknowledged so that people can define their own problems and find appropriate solutions. Policy documents (COSLA, 1998; Scottish Office, 1998a; SOEID, 1999) have identified 'working in partnership, building community capacity and promoting active citizenship' as important ways in which community educators can help marginalised communities to become more socially included. The language of policy documents may be more rhetorical than real but such rhetoric does provide opportunities for community educators to apply policy initiatives in ways that contribute towards building a more equal society.

Working in partnership — parents, schools and community educators
Community education has been urged to work in partnership with other organisations and professionals in order to reduce social exclusion (Scottish Office, 1998a). An aspect of social exclusion that has received particular attention has been the raising of children's attainment and the role of parental involvement in schools as a contributor to this process. One way in which parents can be encouraged to become more involved in the school is for community educators and schoolteachers to work in partnership, bringing together their different perspectives on education. Such partnerships are not easy to achieve given the different purposes that both parties have. For illustrative purposes this chapter will focus on a project based in an urban area suffering from multiple socio-economic-disadvantage.

This project had two broad aims. The first was to encourage parental involvement in their children's school as a means of increasing the educational attainment of their children. This aspect of the project was seen as collaboration between local parents and the school staff. The second aim was to foster partnership between home, school and community by increasing the social interaction and self-confidence of parents and improving their access to jobs. This part of the project focused on the 'whole parent' and provided a variety of courses that were determined in response to local need. Provision for parents to develop their own education as well at that of their children was included and some mothers developed several groups themselves. These included a 'before and after school club' that was led, managed and staffed by local people. Very wide local networks of agencies, including those led by local people, were used to deliver a range of work preparation courses.

A full-time community educator worked with the project and saw her chief role as encouraging the parents' decision-making and autonomy (see Tett, 2001). Much of her work involved establishing and maintaining good working relationships with parents, teaching staff and the network of outside agencies. When interviewed, she emphasised the importance of meeting the needs of parents and encouraging them to develop an awareness of their own requirements. This involved taking time to discuss with parents what provision they wished to see and providing support for them in achieving their own objectives rather than simply meeting those identified by the school.

Parents living in socio-economically disadvantaged areas are often regarded by teachers as lacking the educational ability to make a positive contribution to the school and there is therefore no possibility of them being seen as genuine partners in their children's schooling (see Crozier, 1998). In such cases the intervention of community educators can be crucially important in redressing the balance and letting parents' views be heard. Intervention is particularly needed when teachers ask parents to undertake activities that they feel uncertain about, for example, hearing and correcting spelling. Teachers then interpret parents' lack of co-operation as lack of interest or even hostility but if, instead, teachers start from what parents are already familiar with, such as the everyday literacy practices of the home, then their perceptions are very different.

When schools focus only on individual parents' responsibilities for their children's education parents may feel that having their own educational goals is 'selfish'. It also leads, as Wendy Luttrell (1997: 119) points out, to parents 'doubting their intellectual capabilities, or viewing their desires for voice and visibility as wrong'. In such cases, the role of community educators in helping people to challenge these negative self-conceptions is important in working with parents, especially mothers, so that they can feel confident that their perspective is valid and that the school's perspective may be challenged. For example, the project helped parents be in a better position to be more assertive about questioning the school's practices and seeking explanations for why things were done the way they were.

In this project there were marked differences between the community educator and the headteacher in the type of parental involvement they encouraged. The community educator saw parents as educators who had their own valuable knowledge to contribute to their children's education. There was also an acknowledgement that this local knowledge might be different from that seen as important by the school. This approach to education resulted in some conflict between the community educator and the head teacher because of their differing purposes. The headteacher wished to see more emphasis in the programme being placed on the educational development of children, and thus the raising of their academic attainment, even when this meant paying less attention to the needs of the parents. The community educator, on the other hand, felt that the parents' rights to challenge the school's way of doing things should have priority. She also emphasised the importance of participation by the parents in the running of the project rather than simply providing facilities and courses for them. In this project, then, the community educator emphasised the contribution of parents whilst the headteacher had a clear focus on what parents could contribute to the school.

As John Bastiani (1989: 183) points out, parent-school partnerships usually take place on the *professional's* terms, are conceptualised through professional ideology and articulated through professional language, all of which create barriers for parents. Under these circumstances, many parents experience such 'partnership' in terms of 'inequality, social distance and powerlessness'. It follows that many parent education programmes assume that the school's perspective is 'correct' and need only be supported by parents to be successful and so they have little impact on school-community connections. On the other hand, where there is a true partnership model with joint decision-making between parents, community educators, and school teachers and the assumption is that the school's programme is open to negotiation, there is likely to be more opportunity to involve community members. This then opens up at least some possibility of re-creating the school's programme and mission, in challenging the school's hierarchical structure, and in developing authentic connections between schools and their communities.

There are possibilities for partnerships between community educators and schoolteachers that would develop parental involvement programmes in more radical ways than are currently the case. This requires starting from a position where all parties share the common purpose of empowering parents, where they are able to work jointly and where they are able to build up trust over time. Achieving a common purpose is difficult, however, as professions establish different priorities and have different definitions of 'need' governing their work. Different conceptualisations of values, tasks, purposes and conditions will influence the possibilities for developing collaborative partnerships because each partner brings their own tradition that sets limits about what they can contribute. Schoolteachers and community educators come from different cultures and have different conceptions of education and learning. Schoolteachers, for example, are unlikely to see community development and democratic renewal as a key task, especially when their performance targets emphasise attainment in external examinations. Together, however, the two professions have distinctive and complementary roles to play in promoting the learning and education of children and their parents. Community educators have a significant role to play in showing that parents have an important contribution to make to the life of the school and the community. A parent-centred approach would see parents as people with important knowledge to contribute rather than as 'problems' that need to change to the school's way of seeing things. The implications of this type of approach to 'parent education' programmes are far-reaching and would require a considerably different emphasis from that which is currently common. However, it is a task worth undertaking so that socially excluded parents do not become further marginalised by an education system in which they are already disadvantaged.

Building community capacity
Traditionally, public services have been delivered to the public with limited consultation and involvement. One way of strengthening local democracy is to make it more responsive to the changing needs of communities and to strive to involve them in the processes of economic and social regeneration. The Scottish Office has suggested that building community capacity should involve 'communities in identifying and assessing their own needs, planning and implementing action [and developing] effective participation in decision-making' (1998b: 26–27). For community educators this involves working with communities to help them play a significant role in shaping the type of services available to them and in determining how they should be delivered. Working with a range of partners from both the public and the private sectors has been identified as one way in which socially-excluded groups can become involved in the regeneration of their communities through increasing key services and generating local jobs. This is an important area of work and clearly requires the active involvement of community representatives in implementing appropriate action if it is to succeed.

One problem in involving local people in this way is that the structural difficulties that arise from the social and geographical segregation of their communities are not resolved by those that have created them. Instead they are passed down the line to the residents, who have little power to solve them. These problems of regeneration and collaborative working are downplayed in official government literature, where there is a tendency to present an idealised model about the merits of partnerships. In particular there is an assumption that communities are homogenous and so achieving consensus among the community participants is seen as relatively unproblematic. For example, the Scottish Executive (2000c) suggested that 'Services need to listen to their communities with a single ear. Having listened they need to change the services they provide and the way in which they are delivered in a way that is more responsive to their communities' needs'. In contrast, research shows the conflictual character of co-ordinating different and unequal interest and identity groups, and therefore the crucial question of differential power relations (Hatcher and Leblond, 2001). Thus it is important to distinguish between involvement and empowerment and between strategic power and operational power. Some partners may have the power to set the agendas; some only to participate in the implementation of agendas set by others. In other words, partnerships are characterised by processes of inclusion and exclusion. Just as some potential partners may be wholly or partially excluded, so others may be compulsorily included: projects that are presented as 'partnerships' are not entirely the product of voluntary collaboration. In the case of the Social Inclusion Partnerships, for example, community representatives and activists are designated as 'partners' whether they desire it or not.

Another problematic area results from the differences between partners in terms of their influence. Community partners are more likely to have limited access to information compared with private and public sector representatives and so are unable to make appropriate interventions. This issue is exacerbated by the way in which partnerships for regeneration are implemented. Additional resources are only available for a limited time, have to be spent quickly, and so there is little opportunity for careful consultation and consolidation. Such partnership initiatives rarely provide long-term sustainable funding and often fold with the resulting demoralisation of the community which is left to cope with the fall-out. This also highlights the importance of giving sufficient recognition to the resources that are provided on a continuing basis within communities rather than simply concentrating on new resources that are provided for new initiatives. Communities consistently provide the human resources of voluntary effort and enthusiasm that sustain informal patterns of community care and community solidarity but these are often ignored (Mayo, 1997: 11).

Given these difficulties with community capacity-building how might communities and the community educators who work with them be more effectively empowered through participating in partnerships for socio-economic renewal? Partnerships for regeneration are potentially creative but they can founder unless they are based on shared interests, with agreed mechanisms for negotiating differences. One key is that they must be set in the context of longer-term strategies for community development that offer strategic possibilities for renewal. If communities are to be fully involved then maximum access to as much information as possible is needed, particularly research that will enable them to justify alternative views. Participatory action research is one way in which communities can build more systematic knowledge bases from their own experiences as a counter-weight to external, specialist knowledge. In addition, structures need to be in place to enable them to influence decision-making through developing their own ideas and agendas, pro-actively. They also need to have access to independent specialist advice that would enable them to develop their own policy analysis. Having control over resources of money, time and staff is also a powerful tool, in establishing a more equal place at the partnership table. If these conditions were met then communities would be better placed to:

> Play an active role in setting the agenda and pressing for the wider policy changes required. [This kind of partnership for renewal would then be able to meet] social needs as defined from the bottom up, rather than responding to the requirements of market-led agendas determined from the top down (Mayo, 1997: 24).

Community educators have an important role to play in assisting communities to understand, operate within, and, where necessary, challenge their political environment. This involves identifying and stressing areas of commonality and the creative development of links and alliances between groups that might otherwise see themselves in competition. It also involves recognising the rights of those who experience problems to define appropriate solutions and campaign for their implementation, often against the vested interests of the powerful. It is difficult for community representatives to be active and equal partners in decision-making when they disagree with the proposals of the other, more powerful members of the partnership. In these circumstances the resulting conflict and disagreement often leads the other partners to silence, in effect, the community's dissenting voices by marginalising their perspective. In circumstances where strategic decisions are centralised and generated from the top-down in ways that leave little space for agendas based on local, democratically informed, needs then it is better that community representatives should refuse to be involved. Becoming incorporated into a partnership that seeks to achieve goals that are not in the community's interest silences criticism. A forced consensus results that assumes the community's compliance but masks profound disagreement. It is at this point that decisions have to be made about whether the best interests of the community would be served by remaining within a partnership or campaigning from the outside. Campaigning with the community for their issues to be represented is likely to be a more productive option if community voices are marginalised. Community educators, in these circumstances, have an important role to play in educating the other partners to see this kind of community capacity-building as an opportunity for impoverished communities to take action based on their own interests, rather than as a potential threat to their professional positions.

Developing active citizenship

Community education, through its role in engaging with people in communities around their interests, has been identified (see Scottish Office, 1998a) as having an important role to play in developing active citizenship. Citizenship is a difficult concept to define although there are broadly two main types of understanding. One conception sees it as a status bestowed on those people who are full members of a community with the rights and obligations that flow from that membership. Another conception attaches importance to the social relationships that enable people to actively participate in decision-making in their social, economic, cultural and political life (Lister, 1997: 29). The first conception gives priority to status and the second to citizenship as an active practice. This latter conception prioritises the ability of people who are disadvantaged, in terms of power and resources, to exercise their civil and political rights effectively in order to achieve their valued goals. This involves promoting their free and equal participation, in both defining the problems to be addressed and the solutions to be used, in ways that mitigate economic and social inequalities. It requires a public space in which different groups can come together to air their differences and build solidarity around common interests.

By prioritising citizenship as active participation in the governance of the community, community educators could help to counter and replace the more common assumption that people have the status of either clients or consumers. The active participation of ordinary people in creating the projects that shape their selves, as well as the communities in which they live, provides a reason for working together with others to secure trusting relations within the community. The possibility of shared understanding requires not only the valuing of others but also the creation of communities in which mutuality and thus the conditions for learning can flourish. As Stewart Ranson suggests:

> There is no solitary learning: we can only create our worlds together. The unfolding agency of the self grows out of the interaction with others. It is *inescapably a social creation* (Ranson, 1998: 20).

A community that learns to create institutional arrangements that include the whole variety of voices in its deliberations is likely to be a democratically just community and thus robust and capable enough to address the difficult problems that it faces in the new century.

Citizenship politics can be oppositional and disruptive when community groups prioritise issues that might become challenges to dominant interests and agendas. For example, non-violent direct action against the closing down of a local school prioritises a different vision of what might be for the good of the community from that proposed by the local authority. These kinds of struggles provide a local arena for people to exercise their citizenship in ways that they often find more engaging than broader national issues. As a process this can both strengthen excluded communities and, through collective action, promote the citizenship of individuals within those communities. As Ruth Lister points out:

Such action can boost individual and collective self-confidence, as individuals and groups come to see themselves as political actors and effective citizens. This is especially true for women for whom involvement in community organisations can be more personally fruitful than engagement in formal politics that are often experienced as more alienating than empowering (Lister, 1997:33).

Placing value on informal politics does not, however, mean ignoring the continuing need both to open up formal political areas and to make formal politics more accountable to the informal.

People have the fundamental right as citizens to give voice and be listened to within the process of decision-making. Members of communities need to recognise each other as citizens who share a common status and equal rights but this is difficult given that we live increasingly within communities of difference. Ours is a heterogeneous society with many different voices, which means that people can be excluded from participation in democratic decision-making in two broad ways. One way is by failing to recognise people's cultural differences and the other is through the inequality of distribution of socio-economic resources. The challenge for a strengthened local democracy is to discover processes that can reconcile the valuing of difference with the need for shared understanding and agreement about public purpose that dissolves prejudice and discrimination. People's interests therefore need to be represented in public debates both in terms of their cultural conditions and their material class interests. An inclusive citizenship requires the recognition of different voices as well as the fair distribution of resources that provide the conditions for equal participation. The challenge is to establish an understanding that embraces both the recognition of people's voices and the redistribution of resources in order to create a just, inclusive democracy.

There is a danger, however, that what is said to be an appropriate response to different cultures and religions actually rationalises oppressive practices because it makes inappropriate assumptions about minority ethnic cultures. Failure to challenge such hidden racism legitimates discrimination against particular sections of society and consequently other vulnerable groups. One example of citizenship education that addresses the recognition of different voices is anti-racist work. This involves confronting the reality of racism and developing a comprehensive and proactive strategy of anti-racist policy and practice. For community educators this requires making racism visible and recognising it as a daily reality for black and minority ethnic communities. One aspect of this action involves these communities, who are largely marginalised when it comes to having their voices heard, leading the process of shaping future action against racism. It also must require members of the white majority community to address their responsibility as citizens to understand racism and counteract it and also to incorporate into policy and practice the voices of those suffering the effects of racism. Making the connections between racism and other forms of inequality is crucial if communities are to see the common problems that unite them. As Rowena Arshad (1999: 288) points out 'anti-racist education must speak the language of rights (not needs), of life-chances (not lifestyles), of dismantling structures (not merely reforming them)'. It also involves organising not *for* culture, but *against* racism and the erosion of civil liberties, and *against* injustice and *for* equality, as common causes. Such action for racial justice must begin from 'the experience and the aspirations of those who have been on the receiving end of racism' (Arshad, *op cit.*). When black and white people work together in anti-racist alliances a politics of solidarity can be created.

Communities need to be open to mutual recognition of the different perspectives and alternative views of the world in ways that allow pre-judgements to be challenged so that assumptions can be amended and an enriched understanding of others can be developed. The key to the transformation of prejudice lies in developing an understanding that leads people beyond their initial positions to take account of others and develop a richer, more comprehensive view. Discussion lies at the heart of learning because through dialogue people learn to take a wider, more differentiated view and thus acquire sensitivity, subtlety and capacity for judgement. Identities are respected and compromises, if not consensus, are reached between rival traditions. By providing forums for participation and voice, conditions for mutual accountability can be created so that citizens can take each other's needs and claims into account in order to create the conditions for each other's development. As Ralph Miliband suggests:

> Education for citizenship means above all the nurturing of a capacity and willingness to question, to probe, to ask awkward questions, to see through obfuscation and lies. [It requires] the cultivation of an awareness that the request for individual fulfilment needs to be combined with the larger demands of solidarity and concern for the public good (Miliband, 1994: 96)

Educating desire

So far this chapter has considered engagement with communities that has focused on combating disadvantage and making changes within the existing structures that would lead to some improvements in people's lives. This section draws on the work of Jim Crowther and Mae Shaw (1997: 267–279) to examine how far those with a more radical vision of community education could work with 'social movements' in order to provide progressive social change. Social movements, such as the women's movement, or the disability rights campaign or the coalition against globalisation, all act to critique the existing social order, highlighting inadequacies and offering new ways of thinking. For example, the women's movement emphasised that apparently personal issues, such as the time spent on caring for the family, were actually political issues that required public action. Members of social movements subscribe to a common cause that is expressed collectively and embody a set of beliefs that reflect their shared values and purposes.

Social movements contribute to social change through the politicising of areas of experience that were previously excluded from the political agenda. For example, the disability movement has challenged the discourse of personal handicap and shown instead how society erects disabling attitudinal, organisational and environmental barriers that exclude many of its citizens. Engaging in principled action has also been an effective way in which social movements have challenged the climate of opinion. For example, media images of activists protesting against environmental exploitation and pollution, potentially putting their lives at risk for a wider cause, has forced discussion of these issues on to the political agenda and made the link between the global and local.

People who participate in social movements engage in significant collective learning experiences but their educative potential often goes unnoticed by educators. These contribute to the creation of a critically informed public through the dissemination of ideas, values and beliefs that are in opposition to the *status quo*. Through their participation they become actors in the political process rather than passive observers of others' activity. The important task, therefore, is to find ways of systematising a curriculum that extends what is learned whilst, at the same time, achieving successful social action. This type of relationship suggests a very different educational process from the traditional one where the educator defines what it is relevant to learn. Instead educators become resources for social movements and the curriculum that their members see as relevant to their interests.

The educative potential of social movements is not limited to those directly participating in them because of the challenges that they provide to 'common sense' and dominant ways of thinking. Many movements seek to influence the public agenda by posing counter-positions and so challenging the limitations of the taken for granted. One example is the Zero Tolerance campaign that, through a series of graphic media campaigns, highlighted the problem of institutionalised and culturally endorsed male violence against women and associated issues such as the very low rate of convictions for rape. Campaigning against domestic abuse highlights the importance of seeing the political as encompassing personal, domestic and social relations rather than only being about voting and democratic representation.

The autonomy of groups to define their own problems and develop their own organisational structures leads to a more genuinely democratic structure. The educational opportunities presented by working with such groups that are committed to progressive social change can be enormous. Working to develop a curriculum from the social context of individual experience requires identifying the contradictions that experience raises. For example, the experience of being disabled includes dependency, and the analysis of what this means should be regarded as an educational resource rather than a problem to be solved. The idea of activists as learners also connects with the historical tradition of radical social action that emerged out of industrialisation and the consequential changes in social structures in which political analysis was regarded as a prerequisite for transformative social change. Educational engagement with dissenting citizens poses quite starkly the choice of developing an enriched democratic curriculum against incorporation into passive participation. As Paulo Freire (1972: 56) pointed out:

> There is no such thing as a neutral education process. Education either functions as an instrument that is used to facilitate the integration of the young into the logic of the present system and bring about conformity to it or it becomes the practice of freedom. [Education then becomes] the means by which men and women deal critically and creatively with reality and discover how to participate in the transformation of the world.

The articulation of a vision that expresses the social nature of our experience, which aims to turn personal troubles into public issues and to support social movements that act to transform the world, are therefore legitimate educational aims.

Social movements have also played an important part in stretching our imagination about alternative ways of being because they open up questions about what we value and how we want to live. They ask questions about what type of society we want for the future and thus 'inject critique, vision and imagination into what we have learnt to take for granted' (Crowther, 1999: 36). By seeing the world as it is and how it might be, social movements are intrinsically utopian. In this sense utopia's proper role is to stir the imagination and challenge comfortable habits — a place to be desired rather than a place that does not exist. Community education too should be concerned with the world as it could be, as much as with the world as it is. This might be dismissed by the cynical as utopian, but without utopian thought our visions for the future are impoverished. It is important to begin questioning our desires and to test them against other desires in order to explore what is possible for the future. As E. P. Thompson (1976: 790) commented, utopia's proper space is the education of desire in order 'to desire better, to desire more, and above all to desire in a different way'.

One example of the 'education of desire' is the disability movement, which aims to bring about structural and cultural changes to ensure that disabled people can have the same possibilities, and be supported by the same rights, as their non-disabled contemporaries. The movement changed the focus of activity in relation to disability away from organisations *for* disabled people to organisations controlled and run *by* disabled people. They stress autonomy and the importance of self-organisation as a challenge to the myth of passivity and the objectification of disabled people that results from underlying oppressive ideologies and social relations. As Tom Shakespeare (1993: 263) points out, 'in making "personal troubles" into "public issues", disabled people are affirming the validity and importance of their own identity, rejecting the victimising tendencies of society at large, and their own socialisation'.

An aspect of this change of consciousness has been for disabled people to adopt a 'disabled identity' with the same vigour and sense of purpose as has been achieved in other social movements such as the lesbian and gay movement. 'This necessarily involves the subordination of individual circumstances to a shared sense of identity and experience of social oppression, and a united opposition to a disabling society' (Barnes et al, 1999: 174). The process of positive identification for disabled people is made difficult by the existence of internalised oppression, coupled with segregation and isolation from sources of collective support and strength. Nevertheless, the movement has been an educational force for change both within disability organisations and through its campaigning role in educating the wider world. It has enabled disabled people to desire a better life and thus to campaign actively for their human, civil and political rights through consciousness-raising and education.

Making a difference?

Community educators have a number of ways of encouraging individuals and groups to be involved in making things happen rather than being told what to do by 'experts' or have things happen to them. It is vital that this be achieved through dialogue rather than through pre-established and arbitrary forms of power. The policy areas of working in partnership, building community capacity and promoting active citizenship provide real opportunities for community educators to make a positive difference in marginalised people's lives through their engagement in learning. Educators have an important role in making sure that the complexity of the intellectual, emotional, practical, pleasurable and political possibilities of learning is not reduced to the apparent simplicity of targets, standards and skills (see Thompson, 2000). Finding a voice to do this can happen through being part of a social, mutually supportive group that is engaged in learning. Such learning is a political, as well as an educational, activity because spaces are opened up for the public discussion of the issues with which people are concerned. Active groups can force into the public domain aspects of social conduct such as violence against women in the home that previously were undiscussed or were settled by traditional practices. This means that their voices 'help to contest the traditional, the official, the patriarchal, the privileged and the academic view of things' (Thompson, 2000: 143).

An emphasis on whose experiences count, and how they are interpreted and understood, helps us to challenge the 'common sense' of everyday assumptions about experience and its relationship to knowledge production. This allows new claims to be made for the legitimacy of reflexive experience leading to 'really useful knowledge' for those who are involved in generating it. In questioning the discourses that frame the ways of thinking, problems, and practices which are regarded as legitimate, it begins to be possible for people to open up new ways of reflexively thinking about the social construction of their experiences. When people create their own knowledge and have their voices heard, narrow definitions of what is thought to be 'educated knowledge' and who it is that makes it, are thrown into question. In this way the experiences and stories that have been excluded, and the mystification caused by 'expert' knowledge, can be interrogated as a way of articulating views that come from below rather than above. This is important 'because, in identifying and making spaces where alternative ways of thinking and being can be worked up, such practices increase the possibilities of knowledge — that is knowledge that is useful to those who generate it' (Barr, 1999: 82).

The final chapter will consider if the possibilities for democratic renewal in Scotland today offer opportunities for community educators to make a positive difference in collaboration with subordinated and marginalised people.

CHAPTER 6

COMMUNITY EDUCATION, SCOTLAND AND DEMOCRATIC RENEWAL

The democratic approach is about more than having a voice in services, however important that is. It is also about how we are treated and regarded more generally, and with having a greater say and control over the whole of our lives (Beresford and Croft, 1993: 9).

Introduction
This book has highlighted the debate about the role, purpose, focus and methodology of community education. The debate arises from different understandings of how engaging in learning can improve people's social and economic conditions and bring about positive change. On the one hand, there is an emphasis on the improvement of people's skills and individual capabilities whilst, on the other, there is a wider focus on the economic and social forces that exclude people. This debate is clearly visible in state policies about lifelong learning and social inclusion. For community educators too there is a tension between their concerns to respond to the needs of social movements and communities generated from below, and their need to respond to state policies generated from above. Moreover, the use of the lived experience of people in communities by community educators to build the learning curriculum may simply reinforce the lowest common denominator, rather than challenging and stretching people, if workers are not self-critical about the implementation of their practice. However, education that is rooted in the interests and experience of ordinary people should contribute to a more inclusive and democratic society. What are the possibilities provided by the educational traditions of Scotland that would contribute to this difficult educational task of democratic renewal?

Democratic renewal and the Scottish generalist tradition
There are a number of educational traditions in Scotland that make an important contribution to our understandings of social inclusion and lifelong learning. Scotland provides an interesting exemplar for the study of democratic renewal because, as Ian Martin (1999: 2) has argued, it is both a mirror that reflects processes such as globalisation now at work in most societies, and a lens through which to examine these processes. As a mirror Scotland reflects the current shifting of the boundaries between the state, the market and civil society that 'demands greater democracy and autonomy in order to facilitate a new kind of

settlement between the cultural formation of the nation and the political formation of the state' *(op cit.)*. As a lens Scotland provides an opportunity to see the beginnings of what could be a new kind of democracy at work 'by developing a more pluralistic and participative political culture' *(op cit.)*.

There are some grounds for claiming that there is a greater commitment to participation and equality in Scotland, at least in relation to the widening of opportunities. Scottish policy is diverging from that of England in a number of areas such as the abolition of tuition fees for higher education courses and a commitment to free personal care for the elderly, which lead to a more equal distribution of resources. Participation in formal politics is also becoming more widespread due to a number of mechanisms developed by the Scottish Parliament since its inception in 1999. One such mechanism is the ability to raise a petition to make a request for the Parliament to take a view on a matter of public interest or concern, or amend existing legislation or introduce new legislation. Another mechanism is the seeking of evidence by Parliamentary Committees from a wide range of groups, especially from the voluntary sector, rather than the 'usual suspects'. Recently this has included the Anti-Poverty Alliance, whose members have been able to show the detrimental effects of living in poverty and enabled MSPs to listen to evidence from the 'experts' who experience poverty in their day to day lives. A third example is the Scottish Youth Parliament that comprises nearly 200 elected young people aged between 14 and 25 years, who aim to be the collective national youth voice for all young people in Scotland. The Scottish Youth Parliament meets three times a year, discusses issues which affect young people across Scotland and tries to propose innovative solutions to these problems and situations. A range of youth forums and councils throughout Scotland, supported by community educators, feed information and ideas into the Youth Parliament and these bodies were instrumental in pushing for its establishment. Of course these mechanisms do not necessarily lead to the real delegation of responsibility, nor prepare people for taking decisions democratically, nor lead to greater equality, but they are important, if small, steps on the way to democratic renewal.

Some of these changes in the workings of democracy have been fuelled by the powerful myth that Scotland is historically and culturally a more democratic, egalitarian and open society than England and this new kind of society should be demonstrated through her egalitarian policies. It does not matter that this myth often masks an essentially meritocratic and highly gendered and 'raced' reality, because the 'social reality of the myth is always more potent than the empirical reality of the fact' (Martin, 1999: 3). One part of this cultural tradition is the generalist tradition in higher education most cogently explored by George Davie in his book *The Democratic Intellect: Scotland and her Universities in the Nineteenth Century* (1961). Davie pointed out the need for interdisciplinarity in educational practice and consequently the value of the generalist rather than the specialist, and drew attention to the civic and educational power generated when one area of thought or expertise is illuminated by another. This generalist approach values the expert as part of the community but recognises that his or her value can only be realised if it is accepted that blind spots within the expert view are inevitable. Thus others within the community by virtue of their lack of expertise (which gives them a different perspective from that of the expert) have a responsibility to comment on these blind spots. The problems that this approach sought to address were those of over-specialisation and a narrow focus on the technicalities of how to get things done. The case for the generalist tradition was the need to get to the root issues and causes of problems, in democratically informed ways, before questions of detail were addressed.

This tradition provides the basis for a distinctive vision of a rich and humane civic culture that is relevant and worth working for today. Davie's argument for a democratic intellect in higher education, where non-specialists were encouraged to interrogate specialists, is a vital part of a healthy society and can equally be applied to community education. The belief that an educated community of specialists are unfit to make decisions without processes of scrutiny leads to an understanding that they are, in effect, intellects without democracy. The issue for the community educator is how to develop a curriculum that can facilitate the mutual illumination of blind spots in the sense referred to above. What is essential is to engage the critical intellect of people in a way that creates more rounded human beings and enables people to engage with public issues. Community education is about the development of skills, human relationships and the engagement of people in understanding the wider social forces that impact both locally and globally. If people are to gain a voice they will need the confidence and authority that comes out of experience tempered by study, which provides opportunities for people to read the meaning between the lines and the interests behind the meaning (see Crowther and Tett, 2001). For example, tackling racism requires the expertise of those who have directly suffered its effects as well as the general knowledge of those who seek to understand and counteract it. Understanding disability includes an awareness of the meaning of dependency, which becomes an educational resource both for disabled experts and interested generalists, rather than simply a technical problem to be solved. To live full lives people need an education that can equip them to develop their autonomy and control both at the individual and the communal level. As the Scottish Executive (2000c: 12) has argued in relation to young people, 'Scotland needs the contribution of all our young people, stemming the waste of underachievement, isolation and exclusion which blights many young lives'.

Redistribution and recognition
How might this democratising tradition be used to promote greater equality through implementation of the current priorities of lifelong learning and social inclusion? There are always political choices to be made about the aims of development, and the state is not always clear about how its policies in these areas are to be implemented. These ambiguities at the heart of governmental policies lead to political and ethical choices for community educators if they wish to create a more equitable society that has the values of freedom, equality

and solidarity at its heart. A commitment to meeting people's needs for a basic income, employment, health care, housing and education also requires the mutual recognition of worth, dignity and respect. Such a society would involve both the redistribution of goods and services to those who currently lack them and the recognition of the differentiated cultural, emotional and social knowledge that people have. It would require community educators to stimulate and support lifelong learning and reduce social exclusion through:

- exploring the contradictions of policy in ways that challenge discrimination and oppression;
- developing a curriculum that builds on what people already know and can do but also challenges them to take risks and develop further;
- helping people to recognise that they have the capacity to learn and to generate new, 'really useful' knowledge;
- working on both increasing skills and developing people's critical awareness of why they might not have these skills in the first place;
- using learning to build community capacity and increase individual and collective self-confidence.

Education can contribute to the extension of social democracy but this requires the valuing of difference as well as the need for shared understanding and agreement. The experiences of marginalised communities and their own definition of their needs are central to the organisation and delivery of appropriate learning and other services. People themselves can develop their own forms of knowledge and this challenges the power of expert knowledge to monopolise the definition of what is wrong in their communities and what is needed to right it. It requires a democratising of the relationship between users and providers, both collectively and individually, and a sharing of expert and lay knowledges. As Fiona Williams (1999: 684) argues:

> Solidarities need to be developed that are based on respect for difference: not the solidarity of the lowest common denominator, nor the solidarity that assumes that all will forgo their particularities in a common goal, rather it is the pursuit of unity in dialogues of difference. Such politics also has to involve both the redistribution of goods and the mutual recognition of worth.

This is a very demanding task for community educators to help to achieve. However, if groups simply pursue the politics of recognition without addressing socio-economic inequalities, then they might win social justice for some in their group, but not for others. On the other hand the singular pursuit of issues of economic inequality can make invisible cultural injustices that render some groups, such as minority ethnic communities or marginalised young people, more vulnerable to economic exploitation.

It is at the level of communities that people often get their first experience of democracy. Therefore, expanding opportunities for democratic life should start here where, for many people, they can engage directly in issues that effect their everyday lives. In the current context, however, a good deal of interest in participation may work against democratic life, rather than for it. For example, when community activists become incorporated into an externally created partnership that seeks to achieve goals that are not in the community's interest, criticism can be silenced. There are also problems with tokenism, in which, for example, the one black person on a committee is burdened with the expectation of being able to 'speak for' the entire community from which he or she comes. The development of local coalitions against exclusion such as those illustrated in earlier chapters, however, can lead to the development of a political culture that emphasises the fundamentally unequal nature of society rather than people's individual deficits. Emphasising the importance of redistributing resources also shows that there are alternatives to increasing inequalities that do not entirely rely on individual action. Popular participation in these more active forms of local politics therefore needs to become central to the process of democratic renewal.

Conclusion
Community education as a profession is always in a state of flux, as was noted in chapter one, and undoubtedly more changes are on their way. The work of community educators, whether their focus is on young people or adults, will always concentrate on purposeful learning and education in communities designed to bring about change. This book has attempted to show that community education can make an important contribution towards the building of a more democratic, fairer, society. However, there are powerful ideological and economic forces that seek to dominate, oppress and exploit people and 'the democratic state must learn how to foster the civic autonomy of communities — rather than seek, as too often in the past, to co-opt and incorporate them' (Martin, 1999: 19). Government policies in the areas of lifelong learning and social inclusion provide both problems and possibilities for community educators to help to develop a clearer analysis of the nature of inequality and oppression. In order to do this, the knowledge and experiences of those that have been excluded need to be valued and the mystification caused by 'expert' knowledge requires to be interrogated. Having a greater say in services is important, but being treated as capable citizens, with a right to dissent from provided solutions, is much more empowering and can lead to democratic renewal for all people. A popular curriculum that addresses the concerns of ordinary people and actively draws upon their experience as a resource for educational work in communities increases the possibilities of developing knowledge that is useful to those who generate it. People then act both as experts regarding their own lives and as generalists too, commenting on others' blind spots about the root issues and the causes of problems in communities.

Approaching education and democratic renewal is this way would not be new but would involve revisiting much earlier debates over the role of education, as Margaret Davies argued in 1913.

Even a little knowledge is a dangerous thing. It causes a smouldering discontent, which may flame into active rebellion against a low level of life, and produces a demand, however stammering, for more interests and chances. Where we see ferment, there has been some of the yeast of education'. (Quoted in Scott, 1998:56).

If community educators wish to see a fairer society then 'the yeast of education' will need to be applied to its work with communities. This approach will be based on the notion of community education as a *'dissenting vocation'* that takes the side of ordinary people against the ideological and economic forces that seek to dominate, oppress and exploit them (see Martin, 2000a). Members of communities would then be perceived as active citizens making demands for change with their different ways of knowing and understanding the world being valued as a resource for learning. Rather than seeking to minimise risk, community educators should be 'educating desire' through challenging and supporting marginalised people to define and solve their problems for themselves.

REFERENCES

Acheson, D. (1998) *Independent Inquiry into Inequalities in Health*, London: The Stationery Office

Addison, A. (2001) 'Using Scots literacy in family literacy work' in J. Crowther, M. Hamilton and L. Tett, (Eds.) *Powerful Literacies* Leicester: NIACE.

Alexander, D., Leach, T. and Steward, T. (1984) Adult Education in the context of community education: progress and regress in the Tayside, Central and Fife regions of Scotland in the nine years since the Alexander Report, *Studies in the Education of Adults*, 16, pp 39–57

Alexander, K. (1993) 'Critical reflections', *Edinburgh Review*, 90, pp 29–40

Arshad, R. (1999) 'Making racism visible: an agenda for an anti-racist Scotland', in J. Crowther, I. Martin and M. Shaw, (Eds.) *Popular education and social movements in Scotland today*, Leicester: NIACE pp 279–289

Ball S.J. (1990) *Politics and Policy-Making in Education* London: Routledge

Barnes, C. Mercer, G. and Shakespeare, T. (1999) *Exploring disability: a sociological introduction*, Cambridge: Polity Press

Barr, J. (1999) 'Women, adult education and really useful knowledge' in J. Crowther, I. Martin and M. Shaw, (Eds.) *Popular Education and Social Movements in Scotland Today*, Leicester: NIACE pp 70–82

Bastiani, J. (1989) 'Professional ideology versus lay experience' in G. Allen, J. Bastiani, I. Martin, K. Richards (eds.) *Community Education: an agenda for educational reform*, Milton Keynes: Open University Press

Beresford, P. and Croft, S. (1993) *Citizen involvement, a practical guide for change*, London: Macmillan

Blair, T. (1998) quoted in Department for Education and Employment, *The Learning Age: a renaissance for a New Britain*, London: Stationery Office, Cm3790, 9

Bowe, R. and Ball, S with Gold, A (1992) *Reforming education and Changing Schools*, London: Routledge and Kegan Paul

Brookfield, S. (2000) 'Adult cognition as a dimension of lifelong learning' in Field, J. and Leicester, M. (Eds.) *Lifelong Learning: Education Across the Lifespan*, London: Routledge

Brynner, J. (2001) 'British youth transitions in comparative perspective', *Journal of Youth Studies*, 4, 1, March, pp 5–24

Byrne, D. (1999) *Social exclusion*, Buckingham: Open University Press

Carlisle, S. (2001) 'Inequalities in health: contested explanations, shifting discourses and ambiguous policies', *Critical Public Health*, 11, 3

Carnoy, M. and Levin, H. (1985) *Schooling and work in the democratic state*, Stanford: Stanford University Press

Cartmel, F. (2000) 'Structured chameleons', *Youth and Policy*, 68, summer, pp 19–33

CBI (1991) *The skills revolution*, London: CBI

Coffield, F. (1999) 'Breaking the Consensus: lifelong learning as social control', *British Educational Research Journal*, 25, 4 pp 479–499

Commission of the European Communities (1993) *Background Report: Social Exclusion, poverty and other social problems in the European Community* Brussels: Directorate General for Education, Training and Youth.

Commission of the European Communities (1994) *Growth, Competitiveness, Employment: The Challenges and Way Forward into the 21st Century* Brussels: Directorate General for Education, Training and Youth.

Commission of the European Communities (1995) *Teaching & Learning - Towards the Learning Society,* Brussels: Directorate General for Education, Training and Youth.

Commission of the European Communities (1998), *Learning for Active Citizenship*, Brussels: Directorate General for Education, Training and Youth

Commission of the European Communities (2000) *A memorandum on lifelong learning*, Brussels: Directorate General for Education, Training and Youth

COSLA (1998) *Promoting Learning — Developing Opportunities: a COSLA consultation paper on the future development of Local Authority Community Education in Scotland*, Edinburgh: COSLA

Crowther J. (1999) 'Popular education and the struggle for democracy' in J. Crowther, I. Martin and M. Shaw, (Eds.) *Popular education and social movements in Scotland today*, Leicester: NIACE pp 29–40

Crowther J., Hamilton M. and Tett, L. (2001) (Eds.) *Powerful Literacies* Leicester: NIACE.

Crowther J. and Shaw, M. (1997) 'Social Movements and the Education of Desire', *Community Development Journal*, 32, 3 pp 266–279

Crowther, J. and Tett, L. (2001) 'Democracy as a way of life. Literacy for Citizenship' in J. Crowther, M. Hamilton and L. Tett (Eds.) *Powerful Literacies* Leicester: NIACE pp 108–118

Crozier, G. (1998) 'Parents and schools: partnership or surveillance'? *Journal of Education Policy*, 13, 1, 125–136

Cullen, J. (2001) 'Re-shaping identity: the wider benefits of learning', in F. Coffield (ed.) *What progress are we making with lifelong learning? The evidence from research* Newcastle upon Tyne: Department of Education, University of Newcastle

Dahrendorf, R. (chair) (1995) *Report on Wealth Creation and Social Cohesion in a Free Society*, London: Commission on Wealth Creation and Social Cohesion.

Darmon, I., Frade, C. & Hadjivassilliou, K. 'The comparative dimension in continuous vocational training: a preliminary framework', in F. Coffield (Ed.) *Why's the beer up North always stronger? Studies of lifelong learning in Europe*, Bristol: Policy Press, pp 31–42

Davie, G. (1961) *The Democratic Intellect: Scotland and her Universities in the Nineteenth Century* Edinburgh: Edinburgh University Press

Department for Education and Employment (1995) *Lifetime Learning — a Consultation Document*, Sheffield: DfEE.

Department for Education and Employment (1998) *The Learning Age — a renaissance for a New Britain*, London: The Stationery Office

Engender (1998) *Engender Audit*, Edinburgh: Engender

Etzioni, A (1993) *The Spirit of Community: the Reinvention of Modern American Society*, New York: Simon and Schuster

Field, J. (2000) *Lifelong Learning and the new educational order*, Stoke on Trent: Trentham Books

Field, J. and Leicester, M. (2000) *Lifelong Learning: education across the life-span*, London: Routledge

Freire, P. (1972) *Pedagogy of the Oppressed*, Harmondsworth: Penguin.

Fryer, R. H. (1997) *Learning for the Twenty First-Century* London: DfEE

Furedi, F (1997) *A culture of fear: risk-taking and the morality of low expectations*, London: Cassell

Gattrell, A. Thomas, C. Bennett, S. Bostock, L. Popay, J. Williams, G. Shahtahmasebi, S. (2000) 'Understanding health inequalities: locating people in geographical and social spaces', in H. Graham (ed.) *Understanding Health Inequalities*, Buckingham: Open University Press.

Giroux, H (1992) *Border Crossings: Cultural Workers and the Politics of Education* London: Routledge.

Graham, H. (2000) (ed.) *Understanding Health Inequalities*, Buckingham: Open University Press.

Hatcher, R. and Leblond, D. (2001)'Education Action Zones and Zones d'Education Prioritaires' in Riddell, S. and Tett, L. (Eds.) (2001) *Education, Social Justice and Inter-agency Working: Joined up or Fractured Policy?* London: Routledge, pp 29–57.

Heath, S. B. (1983) *Ways with words: Language, Life and Work in Communities and Classrooms*, Cambridge: Cambridge University Press.

Heywood, J. (2000) *Involving parents in early literacy*, Edinburgh: City of Edinburgh Council

hooks, b. (1989) *Talking Back. Thinking feminist, thinking black*, Boston, MA: Southend Press

Jackson, K. (1995) 'Popular education and the state: a new look at the community debate' in Mayo, M. and Thompson, J. (Eds) *Adult Learning, Critical Intelligence and Social Change*, Leicester: NIACE, pp 182–203

Johnson, R. (1988) 'Really useful knowledge, 1790–1850' in Lovett, T (Ed) *Radical Approaches to Adult Education: A Reader,* London: Routledge

Johnston, R (2000) 'Community Education and Lifelong Learning: local spice for global fare' in J. Field and M. Leicester (2000) *Lifelong Learning: education across the life-span*, London: Routledge pp 12–28

Jones, J. (1999a) *Private Troubles and Public Issues, a community development approach to health*, Edinburgh: Community Learning Scotland

Jones, J. (1999b) *Writing about health issues: voices from communities*, Edinburgh: Moray House Institute of Education

Jones, J. (2001) *Writing about health issues: voices from communities Volume 2,* Edinburgh: Moray House Institute of Education

Kirkwood, C. (1990) *Vulgar Eloquence: Essays in Education, Community and Politics,* Edinburgh: Polygon

Labonte, R. (1997) 'Community, community development and the forming of authentic partnerships', in Minkler, M (Ed.) *Community organising and community building for health,* New Brunswick: Rutgers University Press.

Leon, D. Vagero, D. and Otterbiad, P. (1992) 'Social Class differences in infant mortality in Sweden: comparisons with England and Wales' *British Medical Journal,* Vol. 305.

Levin, H. M. and Kelley, C. (1997) 'Can education do it alone'? In, A.H. Halsey, H. Lauder, P. Brown and A. S. Wells (Eds.) *Education: culture, economy and society,* Oxford: Oxford University Press

Lister, R. (1997) 'Citizenship: towards a feminist synthesis', *Feminist Review,* 57, Autumn 1997, pp 28–48

Luttrell, W. (1997) *School-smart and mother-wise* London: Routledge

MacDonald, R. (1997) *Youth, the underclass and social exclusion,* London: Routledge

Madanipour, A., Cars, G. and Allen, J. (Eds.) (1998) *Social Exclusion in European Cities,* London: Jessica Kingsley.

Martin, I. (1987) 'Community education: towards a theoretical analysis', in G. Allen and I. Martin (Eds.) *Community Education: an agenda for educational reform,* Milton Keynes: Open University Press, pp 9–32

Martin, I. (1996) 'Community education: the dialectics of development' in Fieldhouse, R. et al *A History of Modern British Adult Education,* Leicester: NIACE, pp 109–141

Martin I. (1999) 'Introductory essay: popular education and social movements in Scotland today', in J. Crowther, I. Martin and M. Shaw, (Eds.) *Popular education and social movements in Scotland today,* Leicester: NIACE pp 1–25

Martin, I. (2001a) 'What is lifelong learning for: earning, yearning or yawning'? *Adults Learning* 13(2), pp 14–17

Martin, I. (2001b) 'Reconstituting the Agora: towards an alternative politics of lifelong learning', *Concept,* 11, 1 pp 4–8

Mayo, M. (1997) 'Partnerships for regeneration and community development', *Critical Social Policy,* 52, pp 3–26

McConnell, C. (Ed) (1996) *Community Education: the making of an empowering profession,* Edinburgh: SCEC

McCulloch, K. (2000) 'Young Citizens, youth work, civic participation and the renewal of democracy', *Youth and Policy,* 68, summer pp 34–45

McGivney, V (1990) *Education's for other people: Access to education for non-participant adults,* Leicester: NIACE

Milburn, T. (1999) 'Community Education', in Bryce, T.G.K. and Hume, W. (Eds) *Scottish Education,* Edinburgh: Scottish Academic Press, pp 837–846

Miliband, R. (1994) *Socialism for a Sceptical Age,* London: Polity Press

Mills, C W (1959) *The Sociological Imagination* London: Oxford University Press.

NACETT (1998) *Fast forward for skills*, London: National Advisory Council for Education and Training Targets

New Statesman (2001) 'Editorial' *New Statesman*, 3rd December 2001

OECD (1999) *Overcoming social exclusion through adult learning*, Paris: OECD

Pertonella, R. (1997) 'The snares of the market economy for future training policy; beyond the heralding there is a need for denunciation', *Adult Education and Development*, 48, 19–33

Purdy, M. and Banks, M. (1999) *Health and Exclusion: Policy and Practice in Health Provision*, London: Routledge

Ranson S. (1994) *Towards the Learning Society*, London: Cassel Education.

Ranson S. (1998) *Inside the Learning Society*, London: Cassel Education.

Rees, G. Fevre, R. Furlong, A. and Gorard, S. (1997) *Notes towards a social theory of lifetime learning: history, place and the learning society*, Cardiff: University of Cardiff, School of Education, Working Paper 6.

Ritzer, G. (2000) *The McDonaldization of Society*, Thousand Oaks: Pine Forge Press

Sargant, N with Field, J. Francis, H. Schuller, T. and Tucket, A. (1997) *The Learning Divide*, Leicester: NIACE

SCCYCS (1968) *Community of Interests*, Edinburgh: HMSO

SCEC (1984) *Training for change*, Edinburgh: Scottish Community Education Council

SCEC (1990) *CeVe Scotland: Pre-Service Training for Community Education Work*, Edinburgh: Scottish Community Education Council

SCEC (1995) *Scotland as a Learning Society: Myth, reality and challenge,* Edinburgh: Scottish Community Education Council

Schon, D. (1983) *The reflexive practitioner: how professionals think in action*, London: Temple Smith

Scott, G. (1998) *Feminism and the Politics of Working Women*, London: UCL Press

Scottish Consultative Council on the Curriculum (1996) *The Kist: Teacher's Handbook*, Glasgow: Nelson Blackie.

Scottish Office (1998a) *Communities: Change Through Learning*, Edinburgh: Stationery Office

Scottish Office (1998b) *Changing the face of community education*, Press Release, 17th November 1998

Scottish Executive (1998a) *Opportunity Scotland: a paper on lifelong learning*, Edinburgh: Stationery Office

Scottish Executive (1998b) *Social Inclusion Strategy for Scotland*, Edinburgh: Stationery Office

Scottish Executive (1999) *Skills for Scotland: a Skills Strategy for a Competitive Scotland*, Edinburgh: Stationery Office

Scottish Executive (2000a) *Scotland: the learning nation*, Edinburgh: Stationery Office

Scottish Executive (2000b) *Social Justice Annual Report*, Edinburgh: Stationery Office

Scottish Executive (2000c) '*Making it happen. Report of the strategy action team*'. http://www.scotland.gov.uk/inclusion/docs/maih-03.htm

Scottish Executive (2001) *Adult Literacy and Numeracy in Scotland*, Edinburgh: Stationery Office

Scottish Executive Health Department (2001) *Health in Scotland, Report of the Chief Medical Officer*, www.scotland.gov.uk

SED (1975) *Adult Education: the Challenge of Change*, Edinburgh: HMSO

SED (1977) *Professional Education and Training for Community Education*, (The Carnegie Report), Edinburgh: HMSO

Select Committee on Education and Employment (1999) *Eighth Report: Access for All? A survey of post-16 participation*, London: House of Commons www.publications.parliament.uk/pa/cm199899/cmselect/cmeduemp/57

Sennett, R. (1998) *The corrosion of character: the personal consequences of work in the new capitalism*, New York: N. W. Norton

Shakespeare, T. (1993) 'Disabled people's self-organisation: a new social movement'?, *Disability, handicap and society*, 8,3, pp 249–264

Silver, H (1965) *The concept of Popular Education*, London: MacGibbon & Kee

SOEID (1997) *Lifelong Learning: The Way Forward* Edinburgh: The Scottish Office

SOEID (1999) *Circular 4/99: Community Education*, Edinburgh: HMSO

Tawney, R. H. (1926) 'Adult Education in the history of the nation' Paper read at the Fifth Annual conference of the British Institute of Adult Education.

Taylor, D. and Dorsey-Gaines, C. (1988) *Growing up literate: learning from inner-city families* Portsmouth, N.H.: Heinemann.

Tett, L. (1993) 'Education and the Market Place', *Scottish Educational Review*, 25, 2, pp 123–131

Tett, L. (2001) 'Parents as problems or parents as people? Parental involvement programmes, schools and adult educators', *International Journal of Lifelong Education*, 20, 3 pp 188–198

Tett, L. and Crowther, J. (1998) 'Families at a disadvantage: class, culture and literacies' *British Educational Research Journal* 24, 4, pp 449–460

Tett, L and Ducklin, A (1995) 'Further Education Colleges and Educationally Disadvantaged Adults', *Scottish Educational Review*, 27, 2, pp154–164

Thompson, E. P. (1976) *William Morris*, New York: Pantheon Books

Thompson, J. (2000) 'Life politics and popular learning', in J. Field, and M. Leicester, *Lifelong Learning: education across the life-span*, London: Routledge pp134–145

Thompson, J. (2001) *Re-rooting lifelong learning*, Leicester: NIACE

Tizard, B. and Hughes, M. (1984) *Young Children: learning, talking and thinking at home and in school* London: Fontana.

Tuckett, A. and Sargant, N. (1999) *Marking Time: the NIACE survey on adult participation in learning, 1999*, Leicester: NIACE

Wallace, C. (1992) 'Critical Language awareness in the EFL classroom', in N. Fairclough (ed.) *Critical Language Awareness*, Harlow: Longman, pp 59–92

Whitehead, M (1995) 'Tackling inequalities: a review of policy initiatives', in M. Benzeval, K. Judge and M. Whitehead (Eds.) *Tackling inequalities in health: an agenda for action*, London: Kings Fund.

Williams, F. (1999) 'Good enough principles for welfare', *Journal of Social Policy*, 28, 4 pp 667–687

Woodrow, M (1996) *Project on Access to Higher Education in Europe: Part 1 — Synthesis and Recommendations,* Strasbourg: Council of Europe